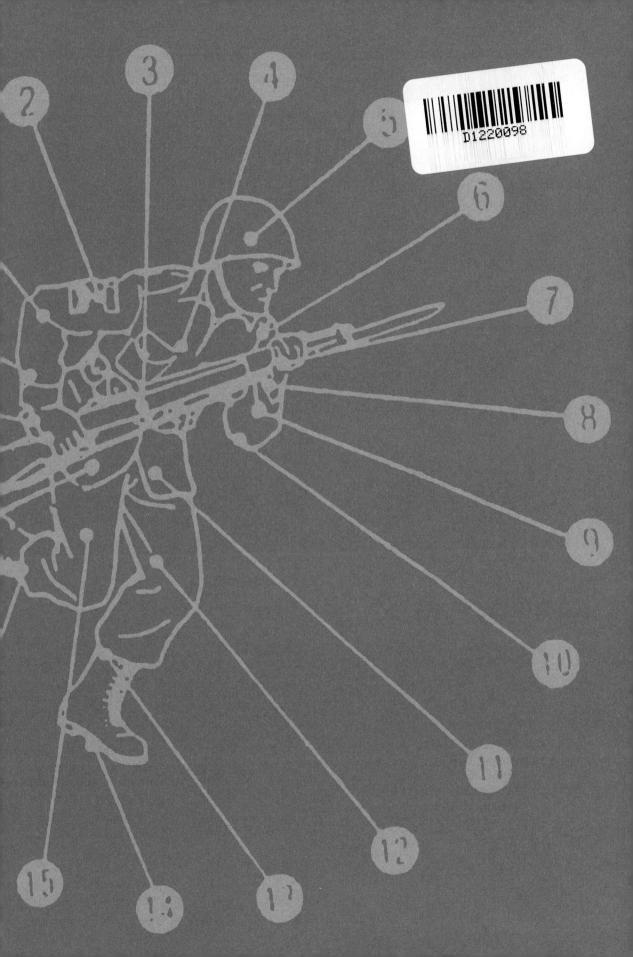

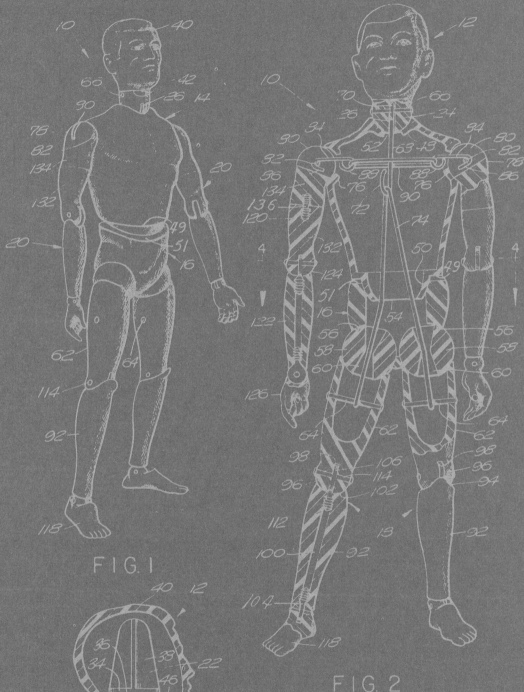

F I G. I

F I G. 2

F I G. 3

INVENTORS
SAMUEL F. SPEERS
HUBERT P. O'CONNOR
BY
Salter & Michaelson
ATTORNEYS

# GI Joe®
# The Story Behind the Legend

## AN ILLUSTRATED HISTORY
## OF AMERICA'S
## GREATEST FIGHTING MAN

BY GI JOE® CREATOR DON LEVINE AND JOHN MICHLIG

FOREWORD BY ALAN HASSENFELD

CHRONICLE BOOKS
SAN FRANCISCO

Printed in China.

ISBN: 0-8118-1484-X

Library of Congress Cataloging-in-Publication Data available.

10 9 8 7 6 5 4 3 2 1

Chronicle Books
275 Fifth Street
San Francisco, CA 94103

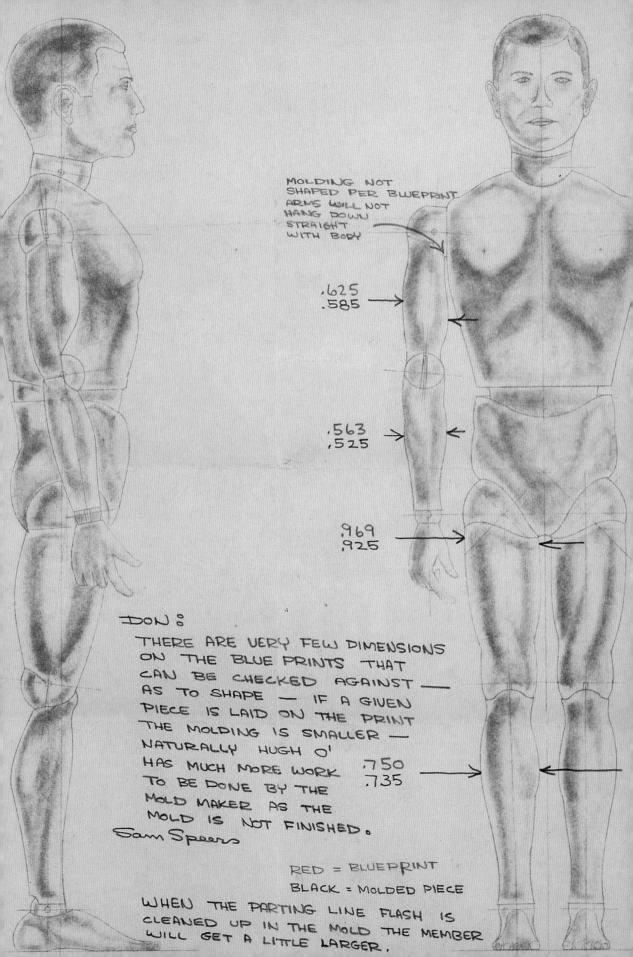

MOLDING NOT
SHAPED PER BLUEPRINT
ARMS WILL NOT
HANG DOWN
STRAIGHT
WITH BODY

.625
.585

.563
.525

.969
.925

DON:
THERE ARE VERY FEW DIMENSIONS
ON THE BLUE PRINTS THAT
CAN BE CHECKED AGAINST —
AS TO SHAPE — IF A GIVEN
PIECE IS LAID ON THE PRINT
THE MOLDING IS SMALLER —
NATURALLY HUGH O'
HAS MUCH MORE WORK     .750
TO BE DONE BY THE       .735
MOLD MAKER AS THE
MOLD IS NOT FINISHED.
Sam Speers

RED = BLUEPRINT
BLACK = MOLDED PIECE

WHEN THE PARTING LINE FLASH IS
CLEANED UP IN THE MOLD THE MEMBER
WILL GET A LITTLE LARGER.

# Dedication

—

THIS BOOK IS DEDICATED WITH RESPECT AND GRATITUDE TO MERRILL Hassenfeld, a gentleman in every sense of the word.

In 1923, Henry and Hillel Hassenfeld created a company in the community of Pawtucket, Rhode Island. Hassenfeld Brothers started small, distributing fabric remnants, but in a very short time they were manufacturing fabric-covered pencil boxes and, later, the pencils themselves. Henry's two sons, Merrill and Harold, joined the family business in the late 1930s. Harold took the helm of the recently acquired Empire Pencil Company, and Merrill became president of Hassenfeld Brothers, ushering the growing business into the world of toy manufacturing.

I'm grateful to have known Merrill Hassenfeld as a mentor and a friend. He was strict, he was fair, but most importantly, he had genuine respect for the people working for him. In the story you're about to read, you'll meet many talented individuals who contributed greatly to the creation of GI Joe, but it must be noted at the very beginning that "America's Moveable Fighting Man" could never have left the drawing board if Merrill Hassenfeld were not possessed of such remarkable vision, courage, and belief in his people.

While Merrill is fondly recalled by many as a shrewd businessman, he's remembered to a larger extent as a person of extraordinary integrity and empathy. He led by example, and his commitment to fair play and service to the community became part and parcel of the Hasbro corporate culture. That spirit is as strong at Hasbro today as it was so many years ago, due to the solid values Merrill passed on to his sons, Stephen and Alan. They each succeeded him at Hasbro—first Stephen, and now Alan—as corporate citizens who seek to enrich the community around them.

Beyond the millions of smiles his toys created for generations of children, Merrill Hassenfeld's legacy is one of responsibility and sharing. I consider my association with him as my most cherished professional accomplishment.

*Don Levine*

**Merrill Hassenfeld**
1918–1979

# Contents

# Foreword

—

**W**HEN I THINK OF MY DAD, I HAVE VERY VIVID MEMORIES. DAD DIED IN 1979, but he left to my brother and me an incredible legacy and tradition. Handed down from an earlier generation, the tradition called for us to be an integral part of the community, to give back, to work *with* people and *for* people, to live life to its fullest, and above all, to take time for others. Dad's trademark was really an office door that was always open to people, no matter who they were.

If ever there was a "Father Christmas" for the toy industry, it had to be Dad. If there were disputes within the industry, Dad would often arbitrate, for he was truly a man for all seasons—a man with a childlike feel for product, coupled with a Solomon-like way of meting out judgment and justice. I was very fortunate, as were my brother and sister, for we had the best of all possible parents and role models.

I remember well the day Dad asked me about GI Joe, and I told him I liked footballs better than dolls. He laughed and persevered. Thank God he *did* because GI Joe and Mr. Potato Head put me through college. It was GI Joe that Stephen first worked on in the Orient. It was GI Joe that sent *me* to the Far East as well, and in fact, it was GI Joe that brought me into the business.

I'll close with the thought my Dad left all of us in a letter to be read after he had passed away. In that letter, he said he would not leave money to various charities because it was for us, his family, to do the giving. He believed in *living* charities. Times change and issues change. Dad wanted us to be able to affect things in the present—*today*—rather than leaving things tied up in *yesterday's* plans and intentions.

Dad left his mark on family and friends, employees, a community, and an industry. We share the memories and the inspiration of a good and caring man who savored life with intense appreciation; who gave of himself and his resources with humor, enthusiasm, and love; and who inspired us all to do the same.

*Alan Hassenfeld*

# Preface

—

I n an age where precious few icons are able to retain their luster for any significant length of time, GI Joe remains a sturdy patch of common ground.

My first glimpse of the universal appeal of "America's moveable fighting man" occurred when I was six years old and moved into a new neighborhood. Coming from a place populated with very few children my age, I hadn't yet competed in team events like baseball and basketball. My new peers, I quickly observed, were avid practitioners of any and all sports, and my lack of both experience and a big brother (two important tools for quick entry into a new network of kids) created a formidable barrier to assimilation. For weeks it was just me and my GI Joe, exploring the living room in a brand new Adventure Team six-wheeled ATV. Eventually I ventured into the backyard where a perfect dirt mound awaited. After not more than ten minutes, reinforcements arrived to help me secure the hill.

To this day I still associate a GI Joe accessory to every member of the old gang; each neighbor kid arrived with a prized vehicle and GI Joe—feeling, apparently, that unspoken access to anyone's backyard was granted when accompanied by a cool Desert Patrol ATV or Crash Crew Fire Truck. We spent the entire afternoon constructing an earthen fortress honeycombed with foxholes and secret storage areas. Satisfied with our efforts, we walked down to the ballpark where I was introduced by my new chums as "John with the GI Joe six-wheeled ATV." Thus ended my tenure as That New Kid.

During a fourteen-year lifespan (the original twelve-inch incarnation of the toy ran from 1964 to 1978), the world's first "action figure" wove himself into the fabric of American childhood. Today, GI Joe is a name as recog-

**Author John Michlig on his sixth birthday.**

nizable as Mickey Mouse or Superman, and his calm, scarred visage is instantly familiar to nearly everyone, particularly males between the ages of twenty and forty-five.

In fact, GI Joe continues to function as a significant cultural touchstone for an entire generation of men, regardless of economic background or social strata. He is a shared

AUTHENTIC EQUIPMENT AVAILABLE FOR
G. I. JOE®, ACTION MARINE®

FULL FIELD PACK

FIELD PACK WITH ENTRENCHING TOOL AND COVER, SLEEPING BAG AND PONCHO ATTACHED.

TENT
ENTRENCHING TOOL in cover
ENTRENCHING TOOL handle
SLEEPING BAG inside pack
PONCHO

positive memory, safely encased in a warm blanket of nostalgia. Few, if any, playthings for boys share this sort of universal appeal. Men offer recollections of their GI Joe-related experiences that range from raucous (comedian Eddie Murphy recorded a tale of bathtub deep-sea diving with his GI Joes) to poignant (more than one person has confessed to pretending GI Joe was his absent father, even taking him to bed at night as protection).

GI Joe has become so familiar in name and form that it's difficult to imagine a world without him. Only hindsight reveals the fortuitous timing that aided Hasbro Toy Company's success with a "moveable fighting man." GI Joe's introduction in 1964—an economically fertile period that straddled baby boomer and post-boomer generations of children—allowed access to a market enjoying the tail end of post–World War II prosperity and the benefits of membership in a growing middle class. At four dollars per figure, nearly every little boy could easily own at least one GI Joe; Hasbro's first-year sales figure of nearly $17 million suggested that very few households were without an Action Soldier, Marine, Sailor, or Pilot. Indeed, Hasbro's current status as a toy-industry giant

is due in no small part to the near-universal need expressed by American boys for GI Joe and his conglomeration of accessories. No parent, acting as de facto Appropriations Committee to his or her son's Pentagon, could deny repeated requests for a Machine Gun Emplacement Set knowing full well that little Jimmy down the street had just received a balance-of-power-tipping Forward Observer Station.

One must appreciate, however, the degree of risk taken in producing GI Joe. The concept emerged in a truly prohibitive environment, since conventional wisdom of the mid-sixties resounded firmly against the notion of dolls for boys. Further, Hasbro had never before embarked on such a costly and ambitious venture. Even the idea of overseas manufacturing represented quite a gamble for the heretofore conservative toy maker.

Yet GI Joe indeed made it to market, the result of a twelve-month whirlwind of product development. Operating with few precedents to guide them, the skilled craftspeople involved in the project designed and produced a major toy line—an extraordinary feat in itself given the constrictive time frame—and became architects of pop culture. We herald industrial designer Brooks Stevens for adding the characteristic circular window to clothes dryers; surely, the individual who solved the conun-

5—Insert small end of tent pole into underside of either eyelet and stand tent pole straight up. This raises one end of tent.

6—Keeping pole straight, put a peg thru the rope loop nearest pole on side #2 of tent and fasten by inserting peg into board. Draw guy line nearest pole taut and fasten with peg.

7—Repeat steps #5 and #6 for other end.

8—Insert pegs in remaining loop of side #2 and flap loops at each end.

10 tent pegs

6 tent pole sections

6 insert plugs

COMPLETED TENT

FOLIAGE

TENT CAMOUFLAGE

Drape camouflage netting over your tent. Cover with foliage from package and any natural foliage you can find. Make sure your tent is well concealed from the enemy.

drum of making GI Joe's footwear easily removable accomplished an innovation no less felt.

This is a book about the intersection of people and purpose. Dozens of individuals crossed paths with GI Joe as Don Levine, in his function as Hasbro's creative director of new products, drove his project through to completion. The varied craftspeople—laboring at all levels in anonymity, since toys don't carry credits—had little or no inkling that they were creating a legend. Most realized, however, that something very significant was being constructed, and their remembrances of that fertile creative period belie the notion that GI Joe was simply business as usual.

As veterans of combat in Korea and World War II, many of the men involved with GI Joe's development found the project more personal than any they had tackled up to that point, and along the way the figure's persona became infused with the varied characteristics of its principal creators. These men could hardly avoid the feeling that they were producing small representations of themselves for posterity, the recollections of their day-to-day GI experiences cast in plastic and sewn at one-sixth scale. Designers, recalling the loyal g. p., were sure to faithfully reproduce the beloved general-purpose vehicle as GI Joe's first wheeled accessory.

It's not by chance that the initial "classic military" versions of GI Joe and his accessories are markedly no-nonsense affairs. Before becoming one of the most famous toy names of all time, "GI Joe" was a label applied universally to the backbone of America's armed forces, the faceless, nameless "grunt." There was no need for lasers or a "star personality." Levine and his staff had firsthand knowledge of the genuine, everyday heroism that occurred among common soldiers in and out of combat.

In backyards and living rooms all over America, we reenacted that intimate heroism, carefully setting up the elaborate twenty-piece Army Bivouac Set, or digging in with the Command Post Poncho Set. Contrary to the opinion of those who condemned it as a simple war toy, the essence of playing with GI Joe was not killing and mayhem. The figure was a vicarious alter ego, and the play patterns it induced in me and my friends were most often celebrations of the ability and equipment necessary to exist proactively while in "harm's way," not the destruction of another group of twelve-inch soldier figures. The enemy was faceless and very rarely (if ever) engaged. We gloried in creating a state of readiness: we

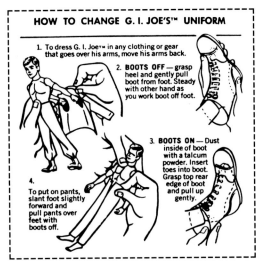

### HOW TO CHANGE G. I. JOE'S™ UNIFORM

1. To dress G. I. Joe™ in any clothing or gear that goes over his arms, move his arms back.

2. BOOTS OFF — grasp heel and gently pull boot from foot. Steady with other hand as you work boot off foot.

3. BOOTS ON — Dust inside of boot with a talcum powder. Insert toes into boot. Grasp top rear edge of boot and pull up gently.

4. To put on pants, slant foot slightly forward and pull pants over feet with boots off.

acquired more and more accessories; we made roads; we sandbagged emplacements; we constructed landing strips; we dug tunnels—while, ironically, the generation in power during this same era worked on the same principle and called it the Cold War.

Beyond the military connection (which didn't last very long; all armed forces–related elements were excised from GI Joe in 1969 as a response to antiwar sentiment), the twelve-inch figure with twenty-one moveable parts was just plain fun. Hasbro's R&D staff could scarcely contain a grin when handling the first GI Joe production samples. This was the classic toy soldier, but freed from a static pose, it was put into action completely at the discretion of the child—or adult—playing with it. This was a toy relationship boys had never explored before, and Hasbro wagered correctly that any resemblance to a mere doll would be all but eliminated by GI Joe's testosterone-drenched milieu. Consumer demand for additional products was voracious—the introduction of an official GI Joe Club (fifty cents to enlist) literally buried the Pawtucket, Rhode Island, post office under a mountain of quarters—and keeping new GI Joe figures and accessories

available became an all-consuming labor of love for Don Levine and company.

My initial encounter with Don Levine occurred in New York at Hasbro's wildly successful First International GI Joe Collector's Convention in 1994, where he stood astonished at the sight of nearly ten thousand enthusiasts celebrating the toy's thirtieth anniversary. At a convention press conference, his grandchildren chuckled at knee level as the media began circling their "papa," referring to him as "the creator of a legend" and "GI Joe's father." He felt a bit self-conscious—after all, many hands contributed to the final product—but couldn't help being gratified by a brief exchange with one particular attendee.

"I don't want to bother you, Mr. Levine," the thirty-something man said as he offered his hand, "but I'd like to tell you that while I didn't have much when I was growing up, I did have a GI Joe. Just wanted to thank you." A warm handshake, and the man quickly excused himself.

This sort of episode became more and more common in the months following the convention as press coverage of GI Joe's anniversary spread. A man sharing the waiting room at a chiropractor's office snapped his magazine shut upon overhearing the receptionist chide Levine about a story she'd seen

AMERICA'S MOVABLE FIGHTING MAN™

on TV. "Wait a minute. You're really the guy who invented GI Joe?" he asked emphatically. When Levine responded in the affirmative, the shocked construction worker requested his autograph so he could show the other guys at the work site. He also shared an unfortunate story involving a length of string, lead sinkers, an "Eight Ropes of Danger" Deep-Sea Diver GI Joe, and poor judgment. "It's still at the bottom of the Providence River," the hardhat admitted. "But I told my mom that I lost it in the woods so I'd get in less trouble. She made me look for it for days."

Everyone from "the GI Joe generation" has a story. As you reunite yourself with the enclosed figure, I'm sure many of your own stories will immediately spring to mind. Because the toy had little or no reliance on fads and fashion, our memories of GI Joe can be unapologetic and refreshingly free from that curse of irony pervading so many other artifacts unearthed from our childhood. (You know the attitude: "I can't believe I used to watch 'The Brady Bunch'— let's go rent the movie.")

This book is an oral history of the creation of a cultural treasure, and I've endeavored to let the story unfold entirely through firsthand recollections of the people most closely involved with the GI Joe project. Their multiple perspectives provide not only an insight into the world of toy creation and manufacture, but a testimony of what is possible when a small group of creative professionals decide that the sky's the limit. To them we can trace the countless small touches and details that kept Hasbro's articulated adventurer head and shoulders above innumerable knock-offs. Those small touches and details are what made their product an indelible part of the national consciousness.

Day after day we outfitted our Joes for impending insurmountable odds. Retreat or withdrawal were unthinkable. GI Joe never shrank from a challenge—countless harrowing experiences instigated by a generation of boys made sure of that. It's no surprise to discover the root of that sense of adventure and confidence in the character of GI Joe's creators. After all, these talented people put the best of themselves into Joe, perhaps hoping their toy would pass along to another generation the qualities needed to face an uncertain future. They were certainly bold, sometimes brash, and always innovative. They gave us an alter ego, a ticket to daily adventure, even a measuring stick for heroism.

This is their story.

*John Michlig*

# One Man's Journey to Toyland

**D**ON LEVINE: When my grandson was about five years old, he announced that he wanted to take me to school as his show-and-tell exhibit. He was very earnest, and as most grandparents will tell you, there are certain requests that simply cannot be denied.

On the appointed afternoon I sat down on a carpet with these little people and began my presentation: "Boys and girls, I have the greatest job in the world. I get to invent and make toys all day long. Can anyone guess what my job is?"

Kids are a little shy at that age. There wasn't a single murmur for a moment or two; I could almost hear the gears turning in their heads. Finally a little girl way in back slowly raised her hand. I pointed to her and she quietly made her guess: "You're an elf."

While Santa's helpers are evidently born into the business of toys, I followed a far more elliptical path. Merrill Hassenfeld, who was president of Hasbro for so many years, used to say that the toy business consisted of many disciplines: it's a fashion business, so you have to be a couturier; it's a finance business, so you have to be a Wall Street banker; it's the advertising business, so you have to be a marketing genius. And then when all is said and done, you have to think like a nine-year-old.

If I knew in advance that it was that complicated, maybe I would have stuck with tennis.

I went to Forest Hills in Queens, New York, for the first two years of high school. Forest Hills was originally the center of the U.S. Open tennis championships, and I remember being a ball boy for some of the top players, because I was playing Junior Davis Cup tennis as a high school athlete. Then my family and I moved to Great Neck, a town out on Long Island, because at that particular time my father was able to buy a small home.

Levine at age 11 (on one knee), enjoying a day of tennis with his father (second from right).

I played tennis from a very young age with my father. We won a lot of trophies together around the country; he was a great tennis player and a great buddy of mine. A great influence on my life. The relationship we had was just wonderful—it was like traveling with a brother, or certainly a good friend, rather than just a son and a dad.

At one point in my life I actually thought of becoming a professional tennis player, but in those days the financial opportunities in sports were certainly insignificant as compared to today. My father came to me during high school and said, "Look, I love tennis like you do, but be realistic about this. You're not going to make a living and a life out of this, and I'd like you to pursue your interest in business and advertising."

**Levine in Korea.**

After getting my degree in business administration at Syracuse University in upstate New York, I found myself in a shirt and tie sorting mail at the bottom of the ladder in a small ad agency. To this day I'm able to give package-packing advice to anyone who'll listen. My father had his own business in Manhattan manufacturing very expensive women's blouses, exclusive things that went to the finer women's department stores. He did some advertising, and I was able to get his advertising account—which wasn't large by any means, but it was an account—after I'd advanced a bit in the agency.

I could see that the garment industry in Manhattan was quite competitive, an exciting world. I became intrigued with the process of design and creation; to be truthful, I liked it more than the advertising. I watched my father. He had to constantly be cognizant of trends and maintain the creative "cutting edge." He could never rest on the current year's product line because there always had to be something new around the corner.

Then it was the Korean War, and I was drafted into the U.S. Army. I was part of the invasion force and found myself going over the side of a troop ship landing at Inchon in September of 1950. We drove the North Koreans all the way up to the frozen Chosin Reservoir and the 38th Parallel.

At one point in my tour—during a particularly cold and miserable part of the year—I was shivering in my foxhole when the company commander asked if it were true that I'd played some tennis. "How'd you like to get some R&R and get time off to go and play in a tennis tournament?"

So there I was, on the front lines in Korea, slogging around; I thought, what the hell, I'll get out of here for a few weeks and go play tennis. I went to Tokyo, and it was quite a different life. I won the Far East Command Tennis Tournament and thought, this is great—maybe I'll never have to go back to the war! I could parlay this situation into a pretty nice life for the remainder of my tour of duty!

After having a good time for a couple of weeks and being somewhat of a local military hero, they shipped me back to Korea with no fanfare, and I was slogging again.

Upon my discharge from the army, I felt that I had to start over in the business world. I joined forces with two gentlemen who were much older than I, and we created a very small advertising agency on the East Side of New York City. We had some accounts, but everything we did had to be split three ways. I very quickly learned that in a small agency with small accounts, splitting the profits three ways really didn't work out.

After the agency dissolved I had the feeling that I'd like to do things on my own. Even if the job was in a company, I wanted an entrepreneurial "something." I freelanced on some fashion things with a few designers, but it didn't take me too long to see that something had to change; I had gotten married to Nan and we had a baby, Sheri, my daughter. When you've got a wife and a child, you've got to go to work for a steady check.

A brief reprieve from the foxhole—Levine winning the Far East Command Tennis Tournament in Japan.

I joined a company in Manhattan by the name of A.J. Siris and functioned as assistant to the president, Mr. Siris. Their specialty was making plastic notebooks, scrapbooks, diaries, and school supplies for the large chain retailers like F.W. Woolworth, J.J. Newberry, J.C. Penney, Sears, and people like that. I not only helped create and design products, but I also went out and sold them to the major accounts; a bit of a nice education, and it afforded me a salary every week to support my young family.

It was at A.J. Siris that I was first bitten by the product-development bug. I decided that I wanted to do something more than just the fake-leather, plastic-bound scrapbooks that were in the browns and the traditional beiges and blacks and mahoganies. I wanted to do something more exciting, so I went to my boss and told him about my new idea: "Ponytail."

A ponytail, at that time, was the way my wife and my daughter wore their hair. I saw it all around me, and I felt we could take notebooks and scrapbooks and diaries, instead of browns and leathery looking things, we'll make them in pastel, little-girl colors, and we'll create a line of notebooks, diaries, scrapbooks, school bags; the whole thing could be called Ponytail.

My boss's response was to remind me that we were in the brown-leather scrapbook business.

I thought about this and figured I'd never be happy if I didn't follow my dream. I went to see some of the leading buyers in the country who handled school supplies and showed them artwork I had someone do for the Ponytail idea. All of a sudden people realized that teenagers, especially girls, had a lot of expendable dollars, and they loved scrapbooks and notebooks and diaries

and photo albums. The response was great—I was ready to roll out the new line! Maybe I wasn't clever enough to get a cushy ride in Korea as a tennis pro, I thought to myself, but this Ponytail stuff will be my ticket!

When I told my boss what I had done, he promptly fired me. I said thank you very much, went home that night to my family, and announced, "I don't have a job."

A friend of mine told me about Standard Plastics, a company in the women's handbag business with all the electronic heat-sealing machines that made vinyl-plastic things such as scrapbooks. They were almost ready to go out of business, and here I had a line called Ponytail that the chain stores said they'll buy. The owners, Leo and Saul Miller, offered me a job; I asked for a partnership. What could they say? We went into business together.

I did everything I could to move things along—I had a lot at stake. In those days large chain stores would give you a test order. F.W. Woolworth, for example, would give you an order for the "A" stores in key cities. The distribution order is "red lined" or tagged, and they tell the store manager to watch this particular item for ten days. I asked the Miller brothers for $2,500 and went to every city where these test stores were located and bought up our product the day it got there. If it was in a town where I didn't know anyone, I'd stand outside the store and say to a woman, "There's a new line called Ponytail. Here's $150—go buy it all up." I'd explain that it was a marketing promotion. At the end of ten days, reports arrived at F.W. Woolworth's main headquarters saying Ponytail had tested extremely well and sold out. We then received a general order for two thousand stores, and Ponytail was on its way!

In 1956, I wanted to get Ponytail into the drug chains, and there was a drug store trade show in New York City. As luck would have it, my little booth was placed right across from a very large booth with a banner over it saying "Hassenfeld Toys." The guy manning the booth was an older gentleman by the name of Al Unger, whom I later learned was Hassenfeld's East Coast sales rep. He saw me and said, "Hey, young fellow, who created this Ponytail line? I see it all over the place." When I told him that I myself had done it, he was incredulous. After convincing him that I was on the level, he told me that the Hassenfelds were in the plastic heat-sealing business and he thought I ought to meet Merrill Hassenfeld, the president of the company. I asked where this Mr. Hassenfeld was located, and he said Providence, Rhode Island.

Unger had a keen, creative eye. It wasn't too long before this that he brought a man named George Lerner to Hassenfeld with a simple idea that had been turned down by twenty other toy companies. That toy has since done very well; Lerner's simple idea was to package eyes, noses, and arms that kids could attach to a potato—Mr. Potato Head, the very first toy advertised on television.

We went to Providence by train—I believe it was a four-hour ride—and I met Merrill Hassenfeld. Hassenfeld Toys was not a giant, but certainly an upper-level company at that time. I was very pleased to meet with someone considered a leader in the toy-business world.

I liked the way he spoke; a lovely, lovely low-key kind of man. Different than some of the men whom I had worked with in the past out of the New York venue. He was a New Englander who was born and bred in the Black-stone Valley, which is where Providence is. He was a civilized gentleman. It was clear to me that he wanted to conduct business in an honest, moral manner. Maybe I saw something in him that was like my father.

I went home and discussed it with Nan.

Not long afterward Merrill called and proposed a meeting between the two of us. Over dinner at New York's Spindletop restaurant, he proferred a deal wherein I'd work for him to create a new company along the lines of Ponytail. He wanted to get into that new and growing teen market.

Again, I liked the way this man spoke. I discussed it with my father, explaining that Merrill Hassenfeld is very civilized, he's a New Englander, he wants everything straight and moral and fair—he's not, you know, like the people in the big cities—and he has a good reputation, well-liked in the community of Rhode Island.

I said, okay, let's try it.

I didn't want to relocate to Rhode Island. My family and Nan's family were all in New York, and I said I'd rather not have to move them to a smaller town. Merrill was a very perceptive man; he suggested that I work out of New York if that was how I felt. So for six months I lived at the Sheraton Biltmore Hotel in Providence, and I would work there from Monday through Friday.

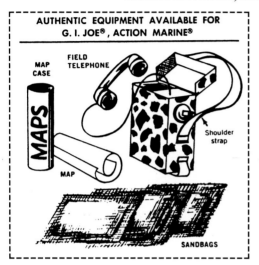

AUTHENTIC EQUIPMENT AVAILABLE FOR
G. I. JOE®, ACTION MARINE®

MAP CASE

FIELD TELEPHONE

MAPS

Shoulder strap

MAP

SANDBAGS

Friday night I'd get in my car and drive three and a half hours to New York, get in exhausted Friday night, and would see my family. Sunday night I'd leave and drive back up to Rhode Island to the hotel room.

As Merrill so wisely predicted, that arrangement didn't last. Before long Nan and I decided to move to Rhode Island. I felt at home at Hassenfeld Brothers, and my family began feeling at home in Providence.

In 1957, not too long after I'd established Teen Time, Inc., my new venture at Hassenfeld Brothers, the company decided to bring all of their divisions in under the Hasbro name.

Teen Time was performing very well, and since our heat-sealing operation used equipment from Hasbro's factory, we were often called upon to manufacture general toy items for Hasbro Toys—like jewelry kits or blood pressure cuffs for the doctor sets—as they were needed. When Hasbro began consolidating its various operations, Merrill Hassenfeld came to me and said that he thought I would enjoy the toy business. How would I like to take over the R&D department and become the creative director of Hasbro?

That's when Merrill first told me why the toy business is so interesting: "You're a designer, a Wall Street Banker, a marketer—but you have to retain the kid inside."

I accepted with very little hesitation.

## Part 2

# A Boy'll Never Play with a Doll

**D**ON LEVINE: Part of what I did as director of research and development at Hasbro was to seek out new ideas for toys. Inventors came to me with all kinds of concepts that I'd consider and perhaps hand over to Sam Speers in product development to see if we could make something of them. There were some individuals I saw on a regular basis; Rube Klamer, who invented the game of Life; Marvin Glass, who did Lite Brite; Eddie Goldfarb; Ned Strongin. To stay competitive, I had to see as much as possible.

Another task I had involved attaching licensed characters to items like our paint-by-number kits. Getting popular properties coordinated with products was a little different back then than it is now. I remember Merrill once telling me that we should do something with Superman, so I found out who was handling the rights to the character at the time and made an appointment with him to talk it over. He had an office over Grand Central Station in New York, and his entry door had a window like the ones you see in old detective movies. I arrived for the scheduled meeting, but no one answered when I knocked; so I let myself into an empty office—desk, typewriter, coat rack. No one around. I was getting a bit annoyed. Then I heard a voice coming through another doorway; "Mr. Levine! I'm in here!" Upon entering the inner office I saw an open window, and through it, a grown man out on the ledge in a Superman costume. He hopped into the room and introduced himself as Jay Emmett. "Promotion is everything," he said.

STAN WESTON: I came out of the world of advertising and found the world of licensing and merchandising in 1959. I went to work for somebody for one year, then hung out my own shingle in July of 1960; the company was called Weston Merchandising Corporation. Its main business was licensing and representation of well-known properties, everything from MGM and their television and motion picture properties to Universal Picture's monster characters, Twiggy, the Major League Baseball Players Association—a whole bunch of standard licensing properties.

My secondary business started in around 1963 when I headed out to Chicago and landed as an account the Encyclopedia Britannica. While sitting around a table with their editors and management people brainstorming how we might license the name and the content of the Encyclopedia Britannica, I mentioned to a guy on my left—who happened to be in the public relations department—my frustration while growing up that I couldn't afford a set of

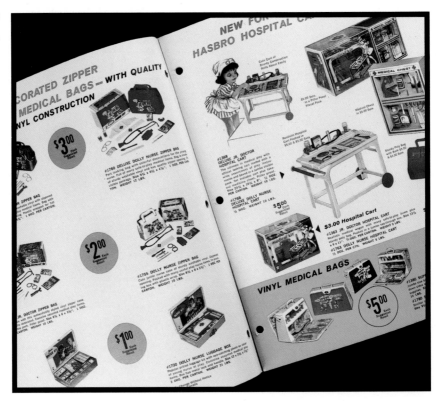

encyclopedias and I always had to go to the library. He took out a pad of paper and wrote something down, and we went on with our meeting.

About three weeks later a truck pulled up on my front lawn in East Meadow, Long Island, and dumped over three hundred pounds of books on my front lawn; they were good enough to send a complete set of their works, along with an entire *Encyclopedia Britannica*, the *Encyclopedia Britannica, Jr.*, the entire set of the *Great Books of the Western World*, and *Compton's Encyclopedia*. So I assembled them in my basement and started at volume one, page one, looking for ideas to pitch to the toy industry.

In these beginning years as a businessman I was lucky enough to benefit from the counsel of Elliot Handler, who was the founder—with his wife, Ruth— of Mattel Incorporated. Every time I'd go to California on business, Elliot was good enough to be a mentor to me. We'd close the door, and for whatever time he could spare we'd talk about what was going on in the toy industry. We would talk products. I remember that very fondly. In 1959, Mattel had introduced Barbie, and Elliot kept on drumming into my head the so-called razor and razor blade idea—sell them Barbie the doll, which is the razor, and then sell them an awful lot of razor blades along the way. I never forgot that.

So I continued through my new collection of *Encyclopedia Britannica* looking for toy ideas. I was tremendously taken by the scope of the armed forces. I remember being very impressed by page after page of colorful layouts showing medals and decorations. So I proceeded to put together what I thought would be an interesting idea around the different branches of the armed services. On my lunch hours I ran around New York, and I spent fifty-two dollars out of pocket at two primary sources; I went to an Army-Navy store on Forty-second Street and purchased a whole bunch of military chevrons and insignias, and I went to the souvenir shop at the United Nations for a whole bunch of miniature flags in bases. I mounted the insignia stuff up on a display board.

About this time we went to Toy Fair of 1963, and I remember toward the end of the event, maybe the last day, going to a restaurant called Fil's right around the corner from the Toy Center. Sitting over a partition in the next booth was Don Levine, a friend and business associate of mine who was in charge of research and product development for Hassenfeld Brothers. I leaned over the partition and told Don I was going into product development, and his comment was, "Hey, if you have anything that may be of interest to me, give me a call and we'll talk."

So I called him a week later and told him I had something to show him.

DON LEVINE: We knew each other prior to this situation. Stan was a licensing agent and represented certain kinds of properties. An example that comes to my mind were the monster characters, Frankenstein and things like that.

Stan said he had a military idea and asked if I'd come see it. He represented a military-based TV show called "The Lieutenant," and he was seeking to tie-in to products. My attitude was that companies such as Louis Marx and other toy manufacturers were successfully manufacturing military items at that time; they had soldiers, forts, headquarters, tanks, and airplanes. We at Hasbro wanted to do something in the boys area based on the military, even if it were helmets or plastic guns, so I decided that Stan may have something to look at.

STAN WESTON: About a week before my meeting with Levine, walking in front of my Long Island home on a Sunday afternoon, I was talking socially with another business acquaintance of mine named Larry Reiner, who was then a game developer for Ideal Toys. I told him I was very excited about this whole military idea, and I thought it really had a place in the world of toys because it had such breadth to it. He said to me, "I know what you gotta do with it, Weston; you gotta make the figure articulated, so you can get him behind a machine gun or what have you." I said, "Larry, that's a great idea. If I sell this baby, you'll be in for a piece of the action."

So when I pitched this thing to Levine, one of the salient points I used in my presentation was the whole world of accessories, and I told him the figure should be articulated.

DON LEVINE: Stan said, "You know, this thing with Barbie and Ken, it's been out for five years and nobody really has anything like it. You could do a doll, call it "The Lieutenant," and I think that might be something to go up against Ken." We talked about how Barbie was very successful and the fact that the "pose-ability" aspect of Barbie was very important, but it really didn't grow on me at that point that we should come up with a pose-able type of figure. However, knowing that Ken was Barbie's "playmate" and certainly not an adventurous sort, and knowing that boys were not buying Ken per se, I thought the idea of doing a male figure for boys could be an exciting thing. I said "OK"—usually, unless I'm so completely against something, I don't say "No, I'm not interested"—and in this case I told Stan that I'd get back to him and let him know. He said "fine."

Stan, I believe, was on Fifty-fifth Street in Manhattan. I left, and in going toward Fifth Avenue I passed an art supply store, and in the window of that store—Art Brown was the store name—was a wooden doll. I went in and I bought one or two and put them in my briefcase to take back to Rhode Island.

Weston—even to this day a very successful guy, great salesman, great personality, knows the business, very creative—decided he wasn't going to let me breathe too much in the weeks that followed. He got on the phone and said, "Hey Don, what about the soldier?"

It started to grow on me. I went to the Soldier Shop on Madison Avenue, which is a very exclusive, expensive collectible place where you can buy military figures—from Napoleon to World War II to whatever—beautifully done. It'll cost you $300, $400, $1,000. Gorgeous stuff for the real afficionado—

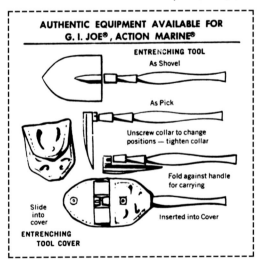

AUTHENTIC EQUIPMENT AVAILABLE FOR
G. I. JOE®, ACTION MARINE®

ENTRENCHING TOOL
As Shovel

As Pick

Unscrew collar to change positions — tighten collar

Fold against handle for carrying

Slide into cover

ENTRENCHING TOOL COVER

Inserted into Cover

the horses are rearing up, and they're hand-painted. They have dioramas where the scene is worth $100,000; the South fighting the North, or Napoleon, or the French Revolution. I started to go nuts in my own head. I became very interested in that colorful world of toy soldiers. The more I thought about it, the more I thought it could be magnificent. I decided that our company would be the company to successfully market this product.

I confided all of this to one of my colleagues at Hasbro, a man with much experience in the toy business. I had a great deal of respect for his opinion and welcomed his input; his background in the industry was extensive. Further, I felt he was the type of person who minced no words, and I could count on him to give me his gut reaction on everything. If we were going to do something as complex as what I had in mind, he would surely become involved because of his experience with manufacturing overseas. The hand painting required to do a doll's head would

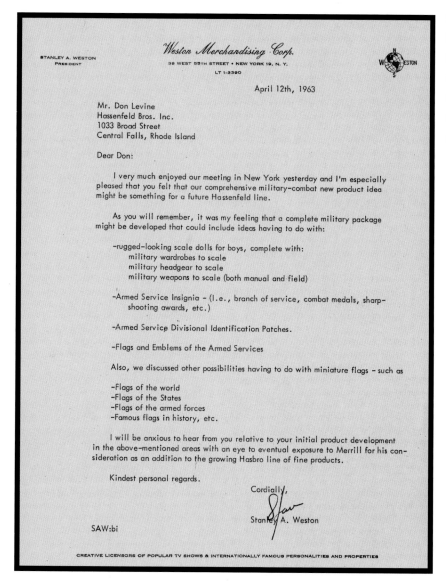

Correspondence from Stan Weston to Don Levine following their initial meeting regarding a "rugged-looking scale doll for boys."

*Weston Merchandising Corp.*

STANLEY A. WESTON
PRESIDENT

39 WEST 55TH STREET • NEW YORK 19, N. Y.
LT 1-3390

April 12th, 1963

Mr. Don Levine
Hassenfeld Bros. Inc.
1033 Broad Street
Central Falls, Rhode Island

Dear Don:

I very much enjoyed our meeting in New York yesterday and I'm especially pleased that you felt that our comprehensive military-combat new product idea might be something for a future Hassenfeld line.

As you will remember, it was my feeling that a complete military package might be developed that could include ideas having to do with:

-rugged-looking scale dolls for boys, complete with:
    military wardrobes to scale
    military headgear to scale
    military weapons to scale (both manual and field)

-Armed Service Insignia - (I.e., branch of service, combat medals, sharp-shooting awards, etc.)

-Armed Service Divisional Identification Patches.

-Flags and Emblems of the Armed Services

Also, we discussed other possibilities having to do with miniature flags - such as

-Flags of the world
-Flags of the States
-Flags of the armed forces
-Famous flags in history, etc.

I will be anxious to hear from you relative to your initial product development in the above-mentioned areas with an eye to eventual exposure to Merrill for his consideration as an addition to the growing Hasbro line of fine products.

Kindest personal regards.

Cordially,

Stanley A. Weston

SAW:bi

CREATIVE LICENSORS OF POPULAR TV SHOWS & INTERNATIONALLY FAMOUS PERSONALITIES AND PROPERTIES

have to be done in the Orient, not to mention the many uniforms and small accessories I was beginning to envision.

I was heartened by his response. Like me, he felt that much could be done with the basic idea, but he was also cognizant of the huge amount of capital Hasbro would need to expend in order to get a moveable soldier designed and manufactured. I began to sense that with the proper amount of persuasion and coercion, I could get Merrill Hassenfeld to feel as enthusiastic as I about the idea.

**JERRY EINHORN** (Hasbro product development): I think it was a Monday morning when Don called us all into his office to discuss a new idea. It was myself, Sam Speers, George Barton, and Gerry Pilkington—the creative department. He told us about Weston's military idea and showed us the wooden articulated character he'd seen in an art store on Fifty-fifth Street. He said, basically, "Wouldn't it be great to have a soldier doll with uniforms and stuff?"

And that was it. When Don mentioned that to us, everybody moved just a little bit closer to the edge of their seats, but at the same time lightbulbs appeared over our heads like you see in the comics. There was an electricity in the air. This was the first of what turned out to be several "soldier" meetings, as Don brought more people into the project.

**JANET DOWNING** (Hasbro artist): Don presented the idea of marrying the concepts of an army toy with a figure the size of Barbie or Ken. It seemed to me that the general consensus was one of reluctance at first, just sort of going along with Don because he's the boss and really seemed enthused with the whole idea. You could hear rumblings of "doll," and people kept saying, "Well, this doll could do this, and this doll could do that." The first thing I thought of was, well, we better not call this thing a "doll" because Mr. Hassenfeld had a standing order about not getting into the doll business. I suggested that we refer to him as a "soldier." A "GI Joe."

**SAM SPEERS** (Hasbro assistant director product development): We had a five-year-old son at the time and I couldn't imagine him playing with a doll. If Don had gone to Merrill and said, "OK, we want to do this doll, a boy's doll," Merrill would have, without question, said no.

**JERRY EINHORN:** We all started saying, "Hey, we can do this, and we can do that." It was a lot of fun, and pretty soon we had twenty-five pages of notes and ideas.

**JANET DOWNING:** Don had an incredible way of working. He always covered his bases and he always did his homework well in advance; so, before anyone else knew what we were up to, Don had us working on mock-ups and accessory possibilities. He wanted to be able to present a whole plan, short term and long term, by the time Merrill Hassenfeld saw the idea.

**SAM SPEERS:** You cannot sell a concept to someone with thin air. Don knew that, and he wanted Merrill to have something in his hands so he knew what we were talking about. We needed an articulated figure immediately to get the money required to start the project. So from the word go, it was "we need this yesterday."

I hired Walter Hansen when we formed the product development department. He had come from the jewelry industry—which is very prevalent in Providence—and he certainly could build miniatures of any sort. He'd sit down just like a jeweler and make guns and rifles by cutting and soldering. With my direction, he began to create accessories and a figure that was articulated.

**DON LEVINE:** I immediately decided that our soldier would be twelve inches tall and dressable. Once the basic idea was in place it was just a matter of mentally going over the uniform we wore in Korea: canteen over here, ammo

**Early concept illustrations showing GI Joe in action.**

belt here, knapsack with sleeping pack on my shoulder, field jacket, boots. We'd need sidearms and bigger weapons as well—it was really turning into a flood of accessories to get excited about. I was confident that there was a way to introduce this new play pattern to little boys if we could make a compelling articulated figure, and the razor–razor blade marketing theory came into play very easily. The whole world of toy soldiers was open to us in a brand new way.

Merrill was in Israel at the time, and I felt that I had a chance with this product if we could produce some good concrete examples of what we were talking about. This was going to be a hard sell, and I needed to have all my ducks in a row when Merrill returned. The first thing we had to do was eliminate the word *doll* from our vocabulary during this project. I instructed everyone to refer to our guy as an *action figure*. Those who slipped up were made not to forget it!

JANET DOWNING: It became Sam Speers's task to come up with an articulated figure, and he went off with his sculptor, Walter Hansen, and Hughie O'Connor, who did our tooling. In the meantime, I was sent to the store to buy some Ken dolls and olive-drab fabric dye so we could make a quick mock-up. Ken was a little on the skinny side, so Walter beefed him up a bit in the shoulders and carved military-style haircuts onto the heads of these figures. We slit the backs of Ken's clothing because he no longer fit into them after Walter's makeover. Meanwhile, I started developing the packaging and graphics for the box and its presentation.

HUBERT P. O'CONNOR (Hasbro associate vice president of plastic engineering and mold procurement): On the 23rd of June, 1963, I came into my office at the end of the tool shop. Waiting in the chair in front of my desk was one of Hasbro's executives involved in the project. He seemed anxious for me to take my jacket off because he had a story to tell me.

So I sat down with my scratch pad—I always had some sketch paper handy—and he proceeded to relate that he'd received a call at ten o'clock the night before from Don Levine. He went on about a conversation Don had with a fellow who said, "Somebody ought to come up with an action fighting man, a soldier, with moveable parts." That's all he had told Don; he had no idea how to get it done or anything.

As I'm listening to him, I'm making sketches on my pad. At the same time, he's picking up the phone and making calls to Sears Roebuck in Chicago and some other retailers, making inquiries as to the potential of a moveable figure.

I guess he wondered if I was understanding what he was saying to me because at one point he looked down at my pad, and I recall him saying, "My God, you've already designed it."

The idea was that the whole thing should go no further than the people who already knew about it. They weren't even going to show it to the top brass, meaning Merrill Hassenfeld. I was told to go ahead so I called in a model maker and told him I wanted an eleven-inch figure with moveable head, moveable hip, moveable biceps, and on and on. He gave me a price and I gave him a wooden artist's mannequin and my sketches to use as a guide.

**GERRY PILKINGTON** (Hasbro staff artist, later art director for GI Joe): We talked about how to package the soldier, and the open box idea was discarded because it really looked like a coffin. A window seemed to be too daunting a task as far as shipping it and keeping it in good condition, so we quickly settled on the box and lid.

**DON LEVINE:** At this point we were working with all four branches of the armed services and named each figure to coincide with the Army, Navy, Air Force, and Marine Corps. Just for the sake of having something to call these different characters someone came up with "Rocky" for the Marines and Army, "Skip" as the Navy man, and "Ace" was the Air Force pilot. I was adamant that we had to feature every branch of the service at once because other toy companies would surely produce whatever we neglected if the product became as hot as I hoped it would.

The first visualization
of packaging for
Rocky, Skip, and Ace.

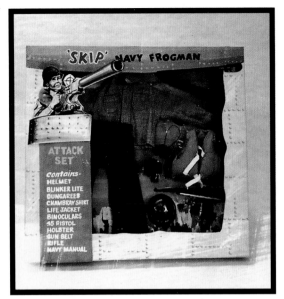

Accessory mock-ups for Skip.

The object was simple; keep it quiet until we could produce some convincing material to show Merrill Hassenfeld. I had everyone sworn to secrecy and we went at it.

JANET DOWNING: We were so dumb that we didn't know there were books full of military examples available through the Library of Congress. We thought we were pretty snazzy in the way we got weapons and uniforms to copy.

JERRY EINHORN: I spouted off about how we needed to do .30-caliber machine guns and .50-caliber machine guns and M-1s and helmets and uniforms and this and the other thing, so as the guy who last left the military—I'd been in Korea for thirteen months, from 1952 to 1953—it fell to me to research the equipment and weapons we'd need to make GI Joe the complete soldier. Don sent me out to find these things, but warned that we were under strict secrecy. "Make up whatever story you want, but *do not* give away our plans," he said. "If the police pick you up, we don't know you. If they toss you in jail, you rot."

I drove up to the Springfield, Massachusetts, Armory and walked right in the front door. There was some GI as the receptionist, and I said to him, "I'd like to see the gentleman in charge." The captain came out and I told him that I worked for a toy company. In order to give him some reference point, I mentioned that we made Mr. Potato Head—anybody who had any kids knew Mr. Potato Head. I told him that we were coming out with a kid's line of backyard toys like pup tents and plastic rifles so kids can play soldier, and we needed blueprints for the small machine guns, rifles, .45-caliber pistols, and whatnot in order to scale these things perfectly and put all the detail on them. This guy looked at me like I was nuts.

"You've got to be putting me on. How can you walk in here off the street and ask for the blueprints for all these small-arms weapons in the U.S. arsenal?"

"Well, we *need* them."

"Well, I can't let you have them."

"Well, who can?" He mentioned the general's name.

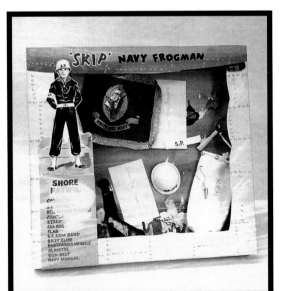

"Oh, may I see the general, please?" I asked without hesitation.

"He is in Rock Island, Illinois, in his office."

"Will you get him on the phone for me?"

"I'm not going to make a long-distance call from here."

"Okay. May I pick up your phone, make a collect call to my switchboard in Pawtucket, Rhode Island, and have them call the general in Rock Island, Illinois, and hook me up to him?"

"As long as it doesn't go on our phone bill." So I called Mary Crook at the Hasbro switchboard, and she made the connection. After about three minutes the general came on the line and I introduced myself and told him

what I planned to do. He thinks it's a great idea, so I press on.

"Yeah, but my only problem is that the model-making department wants to make these things really authentic," I tell him. "We don't want phony-looking military weapons—we need the blueprints."

"Okay, you can have them," the general said.

"General, can you tell the captain here that information?" Meanwhile, the captain had gone to attention in his chair, and I give him the phone and he starts saying, "Yes Sir. Yes Sir. Yes Sir."

Twenty minutes later I walk out with the blueprints to all the weapons.

**JANET DOWNING:** I needed a hand putting together the mock-up uniforms, so someone went down to assembly and asked for a person handy with a sewing

machine. Florence DeLisle was sent to our department, and she was so cute. I think she was very near retirement. They set her up with a sewing machine in one of our rooms, and she churned out uniforms as fast as we could give her pictures and samples to look at.

Mr. Hassenfeld had since returned from his trip, and he caught wind of the fact that a "doll" was being worked on before Don was ready to show him our work. We heard him stamping up the long flight of creaky stairs to our second-floor creative department, hitting every step soundly as he approached. We knew something was coming. It was toward the end of the day, like four P.M., and he went straight

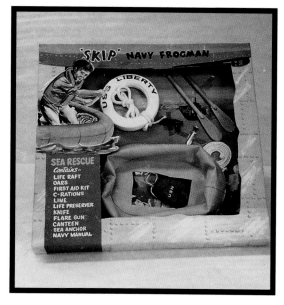

into Don's office and started talking in his booming voice. The door banged shut, and they were in there for an hour while we wondered what the heck was going on.

GERRY PILKINGTON: Mr. Hassenfeld was certainly not a supporter of our idea from the start. Boy dolls were taboo at Hasbro in those days. He didn't even like the *word* doll, so we were very wary of being shut down right away.

DON LEVINE: Merrill got back from his trip and came to see me. He wanted a general update, of course, because it was the middle of the year and we were getting ready for the next Toy Fair coming in February. So I talked about the doctor kits, the new little girls' cosmetic line, the latest Potato Head line extension—but it looked as though he was waiting to hear about something else altogether.

He knew something was going on. I buzzed my secretary, Marion, and asked her to round up all the material we had on the moveable soldier project. Meanwhile, I told him about my conversation with Weston, and how I'd been thinking about military and action toys. Marion brought in our mock-ups, which were in cigar boxes. I lifted the lid and said, "Take a look at this." Before he could throw that *doll* word at me I began my song and dance about getting a product out there that could use the razor–razor blade theory that Barbie was doing so well with over at Mattel. He looked at some of the accessory packages we'd mocked up—there were "Shore Patrol," "Sea Rescue," "Underwater Demolition," and "Attack Set" products made up for "Skip"— and he seemed to appreciate the nearly limitless possibilities in the four branches of the armed services.

"This isn't like fifty small plastic soldiers in a plastic bag from Marx for $1.10," I said evangelically. "This is a whole different product niche, a whole new world for us. This is a *fully poseable man of action*!"

Merrill regarded the crude, mocked-up figure for a few moments, and without looking up said, "Well, where's this thing going to be made?" I told him we could do something that would be new for us; Hasbro could set up manufacturing in the Orient. This was no minor step, since we hadn't done any overseas manufacturing up to that point.

Merrill looked at our material for a while longer, and being a conservative gentleman, he was quite apprehensive from the start. "Well, Don, I just don't know. You and your department are great for coming up with such a novel approach, but this is quite a leap for us. I'm going to have to think this thing over."

When he left my office, I was more passionate than ever about our soldier. As far as I was concerned, we were full steam ahead until Merrill said otherwise.

## Part 3

# GI Joe Is Born

**D**ON LEVINE: I knew that Merrill would want input from some of the more experienced executives at Hasbro before giving me the green light. There were guys who had been around the block a few times like Sidney Lee, our west coast rep and a close confidant of Merrill's. He also sought the opinions of persons with backgrounds at other toy companies that had already ventured overseas for manufacturing.

The thought of setting up new business relationships in Hong Kong and China surely loomed large in Merrill's mind; after all, Hasbro seemed to be doing very well while producing everything locally. Still, I had confidence in Merrill's vision of where Hasbro needed to be as a growing company entering the mid-'60s, and getting involved with overseas production was something we would simply *have* to do at some point in order to remain competitive.

Rube Klamer's grocery store concept.

This was one of those crucial junctures which define leaders in all walks of life. No matter how many opinions Merrill solicited, he alone had to make the call: Was this the right time? Was GI Joe the right product? Was Hasbro ready to jump to the next level?

Another strong concept on the table for consideration at this time was a grocery store idea by toy inventor Rube Klamer. It consisted of typical items any child would see while food shopping with their parents; various packaged goods, displays, a checkout counter and cash register . . . nothing terribly challenging from the standpoint of manufacturing. Given that Toy Fair was approaching, I could see that one or the other—the daunting, start-from-scratch moveable soldier, or the safer, production-as-usual grocery store toy—was going to get the green light from Merrill. I could only hope that this careful man was getting good counsel from his trusted executives.

I was also beginning to form an idea of the artwork we'd need to sell our man of action. I was after real adventure, more of a magazine sort of illustration than the kiddy stuff we were doing for our other products. Our in-house artists were up to their necks in work, so I contacted the Thresher and Petrucci Art Studio just to get some idea of their approach to the product.

SAM PETRUCCI: I remember distinctly the first meeting. Harold Thresher and I went down to Pawtucket to talk with Levine and his crew. They had an artists' mannequin that they used to explain what they were doing and this really horrible sketch of a box; I think it was "Rocky" or something like that. They were gonna have a whole line of these hero-type dolls for boys, and we discussed that for a long time: What do we think? How do we see it being presented? Is it interesting? They wanted to know what we could do with it.

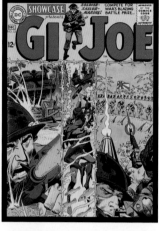

The fully articulated sample, handmade from head to boot.

I had a son aged ten at the time, and he was always playing with my daughter's Barbie dolls. I'd mentioned this at previous meetings that we'd had with Hasbro regarding other projects we were doing for them. It was on my mind for some time. All of a sudden it seemed that they had a product in mind based on that idea.

Then they asked if we could work out some package designs for a boy doll. As it happened, Harold and I had been working on some military-type illustrations for games at the time, so that may have tilted Levine in our direction.

DON LEVINE: I mentioned the moveable soldier idea to Fred Bruns, head of Hasbro's advertising agency, during one of his visits. He thought the idea could really go somewhere but had a problem with all the names we'd chosen. "You're shooting buckshot," he said. "You guys need a target and one direct hit." I wasn't enamored of "Skip," "Rocky," or "Ace" at that point, but the thought of one name encompassing every character in the line didn't immediately make a whole lot of sense to me. What could anyone come up with that was powerful enough to carry the product, yet generic enough to work across all branches of the armed forces?

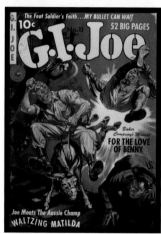

I wracked my brain trying to come up with something suitable, but nothing really conveyed what I was after. It wasn't until late one evening watching television that the obvious answer came into focus. The local station was broadcasting an old war movie starring Burgess Meredith and Robert Mitchum, *The Story of GI Joe*.

Before emerging as a hero in plastic, GI Joe enjoyed a run of sixty-eight issues of his own comic book. Ziff-Davis published *GI Joe* from 1951 to 1956. GI Joe returned to the pulps for a short time in 1964 via DC comics.

Government Issue Joe. The Grunt. Everyman in olive drab. It was almost too appropriate to see immediately—in fact, Janet Downing had used the term in our very first meeting. There would be trademark problems, I imagined, but we had legal guys to tackle that. The tag was just too good to pass up.

From that moment on, we were working on GI Joe, America's Moveable Fighting Man.

HUBERT P. O'CONNOR: After two weeks we called my model maker in with the figure we'd asked him to work on—told him to stop where he was on the project—and he presented us with a fully proportioned eleven-and-a-half-

inch man. He hadn't had time to complete most of the aesthetics, like shaping
the chest and other fine details, but Don decided that we'd have Sam Speers
and Walter Hansen do those touches in-house.

Of course, before we could go forward with test molds and things like
that, we had to get the okay from top management. I'd heard that Merrill
Hassenfeld had taken samples home and shown them to his wife and family,
and they asked, "What boy is going to dress a doll?"

DON LEVINE: I was extremely anxious to get going on the GI Joe project,
but Merrill would say to me, "I've got a lot to do this week; I'll tell you on
Friday, give me the week to think about it." Friday would come and I'd walk
into his office only to hear him say, "I didn't get to it."

Merrill was trying to think of a way not to stifle the enthusiasm of his
young executive. He had the livelihood of everyone at Hasbro on his shoulders. We were a small company, maybe the grocery-store concept was a better way to go. What if we spend all of this money and the action soldier flops?
Why take such a big risk when the company was doing okay business up to
that point? For my part, I knew it was coming down to the wire. If I let him
think about the thing for too much longer, we'd never have a line ready for
Toy Fair or product set to ship in 1964.

The next Monday I approached Merrill again. He sat at his desk, eye-
glasses atop his head and cigar in his mouth, and listened as I went on and on
again about how big this GI Joe thing was and how Mattel would do it if we
didn't commit soon, etcetera, etcetera. In hindsight, I think I have only his

extraordinary patience to thank for keeping me from being routinely kicked out of his office; I was really becoming a thorn in his side with my constant appeals for a definitive decision in GI Joe's favor.

I knew how sensitive Merrill was to the idea of Mattel getting ahead of us in terms of toy ideas. There was real competition there. He and I used to go together to Chicago to see Marvin Glass at Marvin Glass Associates—the inventors of Lite Brite and Rock 'em Sock 'em Robots, among other classic toys. If we passed on the opportunity to buy a Marvin Glass concept, then Glass would naturally take the idea in question over to Mattel or our other competition.

In this case, Merrill knew the soldier idea was a good one that was bound to be stumbled upon by our competition at some point. He made me a proposition: "Look, I'm going to fly some of the top buyers in the industry in here at my expense—Sears Roebuck, Associated Merchandise Corporation, Woolworth—and we'll show them this concept as well as two or three of the other things we're high on. And whatever happens, I want you to be a big boy about it and accept their opinions."

These particular buyers were part of a "fraternity" that we'd consult from time to time. Each came in during the afternoon for our presentation. At night we'd have dinner and socialize.

At this point we had the name, a prototype figure that they could actually handle, and some examples of accessories. We had a couple of additional toy concepts there for them to preview as well, but I had a good opportunity to pitch GI Joe to the best of my ability.

The results were positive. While no one was going to step out on a limb and promise anything—and there were rumblings about the doll issue—some of the individual buyers did take the time to say, "Hey, if you can do this soldier thing, you could have a mega-something on your hands." These meetings took place for a period of time, and I couldn't help but think we were making a positive impression.

Finally, one late night as I was leaving work, I passed Merrill's office and saw him sitting there as usual with the cigar in his mouth and his glasses on top of his head. He glanced up at me as I walked in, knowing full well what was coming.

"Now *you* be a big boy and let's do this damn thing!" I said. After a small pause, he smiled. "How long will it take you to get ready to go to the Orient?"

"About ten minutes," I answered.

## Part 4

# Making America's
# Moveable Man of Action

**D**ON LEVINE: There wasn't much time to savor the fact that GI Joe would now become a reality. Despite my eager answer to Merrill's question, we wouldn't be ready to go overseas until the line was fully developed in terms of artwork, packaging, logos, and accessories. That's not to mention the fact that we had yet to completely perfect the figure itself. The prospect of getting everything ready on schedule was daunting, to say the least—the summer was waning and Toy Fair would be upon us in February.

There was some question at first about which branch of the military we should lead off with. I was still opposed to coming out with anything less than all four—Army, Navy, Air Force, and Marines—right off the bat. Why leave a hole in the market for some other toy company? Despite the short time we had to complete an entire detailed line, I got Merrill to agree to launch everything at once.

SAM SPEERS: Before working at Hasbro, I had run a ceramics plant for a while and knew of a freelance sculptor named Phil Kraczkowski to whom I'd planned to give some work. That opportunity never arose, but I enjoyed talking to Phil and we became friendly.

When it came time to create a head for GI Joe, I called him up and asked if he'd be interested. Then Don asked if I'd take him to meet Phil so he would know who was doing the face.

**A production mold for GI Joe's head.**

PHIL KRACZKOWSKI: Two executives from Hasbro came right down to the farm to see me. They told me they'd heard that I did a lot of portraits. I imagine they wanted a guy that could do heads and faces.

They explained that they didn't like what had been done for this project up to that point. I asked them exactly what they wanted, and they said they would like a young, good-looking American man. I said, "Okay, that's no problem," and actually I didn't even give it much thought. It wasn't a big deal at all because I was used to doing faces and things. I did famous people. I did the life-size busts of Lowell Thomas and General Curtis LeMay, the Kennedy-

Johnson inaugural medal, the Johnson-Humphrey inaugural medal. I had three sittings with J. Edgar Hoover for a life-size bust. Went to the White House to meet Lady Bird. I'm the most successful dropout the Rhode Island School of Design ever had.

The Hasbro people also asked me how long it would take and couldn't get over the fact that I said I'd do it in ten days. They said other sculptors had taken up to three months on heads they weren't even going to use.

The head had to fit a certain doll; I said okay. They did *not* tell me it was going to be a GI, which didn't matter. Mainly I was to do a good-looking head for them. The requirements were that it had to be a young American male, and it had to fit on a certain neck size—that's all.

SAM SPEERS: Phil lived on a farm in Attleboro, Massachusetts, so Don and I drove out there to meet with him dressed in our suits and ties. When we walked in his kitchen door, Phil introduced us to his dad, who then asked him, "Are these the men that came to shovel the manure?"

PHIL KRACZKOWSKI: The head and figure had to be in proportion. It could not be sculpted at an enlarged size; it had to be done at the actual dimensions.

I made the original model in clay and had to factor in shrinkage as it became the finished product. I made a mold around the clay, which shrank very slightly. That mold was in sections, like two halves. You take it apart, you pull out the clay and throw that clay away; there's no way to save it because it never hardens and solidifies. I put the two halves together again to create a cavity inside, then poured a plastic material in there. That became the master, which I cleaned up. There was also a little bit of shrinkage at that stage.

Apparently it was perfect. I told them the truth and I actually did have the head ready before the ten days were up, and they accepted it.

People ask where my ideas come from. I say "from living so long." I've observed an awful lot of people, and I draw from that. In the case of GI Joe, I never sketched anything out and I couldn't use myself as a model because I'm not that handsome. Like a lot of the things I've sculpted, GI Joe came from within. I don't know how these things happen, but I just let the clay develop and when it ends up where I'm happy, that's it. Does GI Joe look a bit like John Kennedy? I'd done the Kennedy medal in 1961 and other full busts of him preceding the GI Joe project, so maybe the resemblance got in there subconsciously. I was thinking of a composite of people I'd known.

I made six hundred dollars on the project—pretty good money. My first and last toy job.

HAROLD THRESHER: A while after our first meeting, Levine said he had a proposition for our art studio and decided he was going to try us out. He came up to Chelsea, Massachusetts, where the Forbes Lithograph Company was located. Sam Petrucci and I both worked for them for many years, and

then they went out of business. Diamond National took over and we were given space there, a studio where we were to do their work when they needed it and work on any outside jobs at our own desire.

When Levine first saw the place he was quite leery. He saw Diamond National printing salesmen coming in and out, and he didn't want to talk about anything there so we went out to a tavern nearby for lunch. We sat down in a booth and we talked at length about what he had in mind; later he sent forms for us to sign which gave them assurance that we wouldn't say anything to anyone about what we were doing. Very secretive about this whole thing.

An important point he made repeatedly was that this would be an "action toy," and there had to be "excitement" and "play value," so we had to get as much blood and thunder into our illustrations as possible.

DON LEVINE: While the outside artists started on package paintings, Sam Speers came in and out of my office with limb after limb of our soldier. Between myself, Sam, and sculptor Walter Hansen, we'd get the forearm the way we liked it, then I'd say, "Okay, let's get an elbow joint made that we can add to this." Next, Sam would take the parts back to Hughie O'Connor so he could figure out the most efficient injection-mold design for each part. My father told me that, in the women's garment business, it was the guy creating the cutting patterns for the fabric who made the profit for the company because that person could come up with a layout with the least waste to it. That was Hughie's genius. He could look at a hand and say, for example, "If we're going to do this on an eighteen-inch press I have to make sure we mold one thousand of them on a sprue; that's four cents per hand. If I get five hundred on a sprue, this hand will run six cents per item."

The bottom line was to make our figure as moveable and flexible as it could possibly be. We went segment by segment on that body, struggling to make sure everything worked together. The littlest things had to be thought up from scratch: What should a hand look like so it can hold tools and weapons but not snag when putting a shirt on? How can we get GI Joe to stand on his own but still flex easily? What do we do about the hips so he can sit properly? How do we accommodate the larger seams on miniature uniforms while still maintaining a "scale" look?

SAM SPEERS: The question came up as to how natural we were going to make his crotch. Some people suggested trunks, but we were going full-speed ahead and didn't have much time to think about it. We left him "blank."

DON LEVINE: One thing we didn't have problems with, thanks to some good connections, was research material. Merrill had a high school buddy named Lenny Holland, who happened to be the adjutant general of the National Guard. During the Jewish holidays, a man named Sam Trachtenberg would make special meals for the executives; 98 percent of Hasbro's execs were Jewish. General Holland would be invited to these holiday meals and pull up in a car with the red panel and stars. Once Merrill had green-lighted GI Joe, I mentioned that we'd need to see a real .45, tripods, and general military hardware to do the accessories with all the detail we desired. He put in a call to his old buddy General Holland; and, even though Merrill couldn't tell his friend exactly what we were working on, we got an invitation to come down to the armory.

Jerry Einhorn had been acquiring military material by hook or by crook up until that point. When he and I went to the armory and saw the cannons, antiaircraft guns, and tanks, we were like kids in a candy store. General Holland came out of his office to greet us and said, "Take what you want." Jerry and I looked at each other and both knew exactly what we needed to do: We excused ourselves and went back to our Central Falls building for a *truck*!

JANET DOWNING: Pretty soon we had weapons parading into our department on a regular basis. We were on the second floor, and the administrative people were on the large first floor. As bazookas, rifles, and grenades started coming through on their way up the stairway to the creative department, the secretaries' eyes got very large indeed!

Norman Jacques from engineering was in our department because he had drafting skills, and he took down all the specifications as the material came in so we could duplicate them in miniature.

My husband at the time was a member of the National Guard, and he said the guardsmen would get so mad because they would have to clean all of this equipment when it was returned. Dust and clay got all over the place.

JERRY EINHORN: Having access to the National Guard's armory made

Lead castings of accessories made in-house for visualization purposes. Sam Speers later found them useful in his tackle box.

my life a little easier, but not by much. We were still under secrecy, so even though General Holland was letting us walk out with guns and ammo he really didn't know what we were doing. No one was to breathe a word of what we were creating to anyone outside the department. Don's fear was that this soldier was such a natural for Mattel that they would rush out a product just like GI Joe if they had any idea that we planned a moveable fighting man. I remember him saying, "Don't even tell your family what's up—loose lips sink ships."

After I'd been working on the project for about six months—going here and there, picking up uniforms and guns and artillery—there was a company longevity awards dinner. Since my wife and I lived near Don's house, we picked them up on the way to the event. On the way home Don started talking about GI Joe—I was startled! I said, "Don! There are civilians in the car!" My wife, Doris, didn't know anything about GI Joe. Don laughed, "You mean he's been running around the country for six months and he never told you what it was for?"

Hell, it proved a point: I could keep a secret!

When we were doing the Marine and stuff, we needed to have equipment: helmets, uniforms, boots, ammo—everything. I made a series of phone calls, and somebody told me, strange as it may seem, that there was a guy who had a warehouse on the waterfront in Chelsea, Massachusetts, who was selling all surplus to armies in South America—because back then, every twenty-one days there was a new revolution in a South American country. I found out where this place was, got into my car, drove up to Boston and over the bridge to Chelsea, found the warehouse, walked in, and there are mounds and mounds of uniforms, boots, helmets, and everything. A guy comes out of some dark corner and says, "Can I help you?" And I said, "Yeah, I'd like to buy some of this stuff."

"What do you need it for?"

I said, "Well, I'm a collector. I have a museum in South County in Rhode Island and we want to do some World War II dioramas. You know, we're building mannequins and putting the uniforms on them, so it will be a historical situation."

He says, "Hey, what a great idea, what do you want?"

So I was walking through the place, and I picked out uniforms and helmets, mortar rounds, 3.5 bazooka shells, hand grenades, machetes that still had blood on them, boots, uniforms; Marines, Air Force, Navy, everything. The car I was driving was a 1961 Dodge Lancer, which was like the first of the compact cars, and I opened up the trunk and we filled it, stuffing everything in there. Grease guns, ammunition, helmets, and hand grenades; everything stuffed into the trunk.

I said, "What do I owe you?" He says, "Ah, give me twenty bucks."

Now this was in 1963. I had moved to Rhode Island in 1955. I'd only been up to Boston maybe three or four times. I did not know the Boston area at all like I do now, but I tried to go back the way I came. I got up on the expressway and found myself in downtown Boston. I don't know how or why, but I did. And I made an illegal left turn.

There was a policeman right on the corner. He motions me to the curb and comes over. I say, "Officer, what's my offense?" He says, "You made an illegal left turn. Didn't you see the sign back there, 'No Left Turn'?"

"Sir, I'm lost. I don't know where I am—I want to go to Rhode Island. I came up to Chelsea and I was on the expressway and somehow I got off the expressway and I'm lost."

He's looking at me and he's looking at me. Finally he says, "Can I have your license and registration?" He walks around the back of the car and puts his foot up on the rear bumper. Being a small car, the weight shifted and something clanked inside the trunk.

Now, at that moment the thing that flashes in my mind is this: That very, very morning, the Boston newspapers, both the *Globe* and the *Record*

*American,* had come out with a story about a group out of Harvard University called Alpha 66. They were sending equipment and ammunition and arms to insurgents in Cuba. And there I sit—and the policeman hears this clunk.

All the while I'm thinking of what Don told me: "Don't tell a soul. If the cops pick you up, we don't know you."

The policeman asks me to open the trunk, and lo and behold, what does he see? Hand grenades, mortar shells, helmets, and uniforms.

"What are you doing with that?" I give him the story about being on the board of directors of a museum in Narragansett, Rhode Island, which is in South County, the University of Rhode Island, and we're putting together a wing dedicated to World War II, and I had just picked up these things in an Army-Navy store.

And you know, I talked my way out of it—I never even got the ticket! "Be careful how you drive," the cop said. When I got back to Rhode Island and told Don and everyone this story, they just roared. They fell on the floor laughing.

SAM SPEERS: We were working to make samples that would be sent overseas for duplication and manufacturing. Walter was carving, and Norman constructed miniature equipment from polystyrene sheet plastic cemented together with methylene chloride.

Since Walter was from the jewelry business, he could sit down and manufacture these beautiful brass miniatures with his little Dremel tools and some cutting, sanding, and soldering. Enormous amounts of detail. Those one-of-a-kind prototypes would be sent to a jewelry company for casting. The models were put between two round rubber plates, which were then vulcanized and made hard by heat and pressure. Then they'd take the two plates apart and remove Walter's models so cavities remained. A groove was run from the center of the rubber plates into those cavities, and then the mold was put into a machine. Lead was poured into the center of the machine as it spun, and centrifugal force threw the lead into the mold's cavity, so you would get very, very fine reproductions of the original prototypes.

Eventually these items would be plastic-injection molded, but we used the lead copies to lay out packages and create display mock-ups for Toy Fair. Being a frugal New Englander, I later put many of the lead pieces in my tackle box to use as fishing sinkers.

Florence Delisle helped our department create the outfits and uniforms. She was a wonderful woman from the plant, always cheerful, and she really

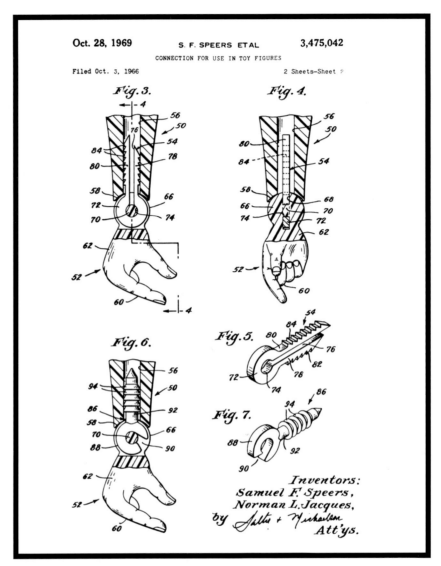

Oct. 28, 1969     S. F. SPEERS ET AL     3,475,042

CONNECTION FOR USE IN TOY FIGURES

Filed Oct. 3, 1966         2 Sheets—Sheet 2

*Fig. 3.*             *Fig. 4.*

*Fig. 6.*          *Fig. 5.*

*Fig. 7.*

Inventors:
Samuel F. Speers,
Norman L. Jacques,
by Salter + Michaelson Att'ys.

seemed to enjoy the work. She couldn't do these things during the day because of her regular plant work, so she'd take material home at night or over weekends to get them sewn for us. We'd give her a full-sized poncho and she'd come back with a miniature version. She lived in Woonsocket, not too far from my house, so often I'd drop by to pick up some finished outfits. If it was that time of the year, she'd make me take a basket of tomatoes as well.

DON LEVINE: I was about ready to head overseas for my second visit to the Orient; of course, under far better circumstances than my first trip there as a GI. Someone else from Hasbro had gone ahead, and he began making contacts so we'd have factories and labor ready to go in a short time.

As I prepared material in Pawtucket, we were firing on all cylinders. Sam, Hughie, and Walter were still wrestling with perfecting the body of our guy, making it able to move every way a real soldier could. At the same

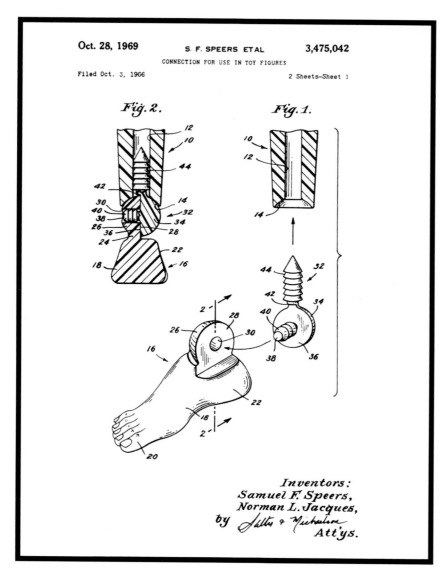

Oct. 28, 1969          S. F. SPEERS ET AL          3,475,042
              CONNECTION FOR USE IN TOY FIGURES

Filed Oct. 3, 1966                    2 Sheets—Sheet 1

*Fig. 2.*          *Fig. 1.*

Inventors:
*Samuel F. Speers,*
*Norman L. Jacques,*
by *Salter & Michaelson*
                    *Att'ys.*

GI Joe's wrist and ankle fastening systems were based on a nail Sam Speers noticed in a hardware store.

time, they labored to create small versions of everything the Pentagon could imagine. I met with Norman Jacques, our box man, and told him to look at the way Barbie packages were made and try to do better. He could take a hunk of cardboard and tell you where all the scoring and tabs needed to be in order to make a perfect presentation. We'd go back and forth over details; I'd ask for more panel room on our accessory boxes, and he'd find some magic combination that made it suddenly happen without having to use more cardboard.

One thing I wasn't interested in was the traditional blister pack, which was the transparent plastic shell or form used by the majority of the toy business. It made everything inside look like plastic junk in a Cracker Jack box. We were developing some great stuff, and I wanted a gorgeous presentation that would show everything off, from the biggest bazooka to the smallest grenade. This was not a case of "great box; so-so product"—I wanted kids

**GI JOE**
ACTION MARINE
by HASBRO®

An

1. Your mine
battery into
positive end
makes good

**DEMOLITION**
mine detector
carrying case
head set · voltmeter
battery pack
detection light
land mines

**GI JOE**
ACTION SAILOR
by HASBRO®

**GI JOE**
ACTION PILOT
by HASBRO®

SURVIVAL
LIFE RAFT SET

SCRAMBLE
FLIGHT SET

**GI JOE**
ACTION PILOT

America's
*movable*
fighting man

**SEA RESCUE**
life raft · oar
flare gun
anchor
rope
knife & scabbard

MOVE G.I. JOE INTO

Artists worked
from photos in
order to create
exciting packages.

and parents to pick up a GI Joe package in their local toy department and see exactly what awaited them.

I ended up settling on three main package types: highly illustrated boxes with lids for individual figures; flatter square accessory "frames" with an illustration on the left side and cellophane fronts so the items could be easily seen; and standard military-branch-specific cards upon which items would be shrink-wrapped.

The shrink-wrapping process was not an easy one. It took a lot of trial and error to determine how tight we could wrap our cards without buckling, and bulky items like a helmet would cause the wrap to pucker and obscure everything else in the package. It was a tough nut to crack. After meetings in my office, the packaging guys would go back to their area cursing the day they ever met me.

Now that we knew what areas of the packages needed to be illustrated, I could go back to Thresher and Petrucci and have them start creating visuals and a logo. The artwork was crucial; 90 percent of the package would be covered with it.

**HAROLD THRESHER:** Levine came back to us with package mock-ups and gave us our marching orders to get it done. I think we had a simple construction that showed how the box would fold and how it would slope around the edges. There would be a frame-like device around part of it that would slope in to the materials being shown. One panel on the left-hand side would be perhaps two and a half or three inches wide and could contain the illustrated figure.

Then we decided what to do for the backgrounds. We had a lot of light yellow and tan wood-grain-style paper around the studio, so we used that and Don seemed to like it. We made a bunch of bullet holes in it, between the lettering and so on. We still have a lot of that wood-grain paper left over.

The package was thick enough so it could carry lettering on the edge. There was a panel on the top where we indicated by color the particular costume group featured in the box. They liked that, and we carried that out for all of the packages.

We figured the guy would be naturally dark; he would have dark hair and he would have sort of a beard—not too much at first—like you would find on soldiers in the field because they couldn't always shave every day. The guy had to look like a real he-man type, always scowling or looking tough. He couldn't look like a weak little Sunday school teacher.

Anyone that we could find would pose for our GI Joe illustrations. We conned some fellows into it and they were delighted to do it for us. If we didn't have the regular Army stuff, we'd have the model put trousers on and we'd give him some boots and simply paint in the olive-drab coloration that was used at that time.

I remember going out to the local National Guard armory to ask if they had anything I could borrow from them. One of them gave me a .45 Colt revolver, which he should never have done. We used it anyway in the leather holster we had, which added authenticity to anything we did.

Sam posed for some of the pictures. In fact, he was the basis of the Japanese soldier in the foreign soldiers series that we did later in 1965. He had a good figure and I was too fat, no good as a model. We tried to get fellows that seemed to be the type that we had in mind and then we diddled it up from there. It was also handy going to some of the photo places and picking up prints of action soldiers from films like *The Longest Day*. They had a lot of photographs of soldiers charging and throwing grenades.

**SAM PETRUCCI:** We had a fella named Lindy Gallegda pose for many of the soldier items. He was a printer, kind of a handsome guy—he was a soldier.

My brother-in-law was the model for two or three of the Navy items. A very sad thing; one of the boxes was a Navy rescue type of thing, and he posed for it in a rubber raft. Right after the painting was done he drowned in an accident. It was unbelievable. Twenty years old, and the box wasn't even out yet when it happened.

HAROLD THRESHER: For the logo, Don said he wanted to incorporate the figure, but real masculine and exciting, like he had really been through a lot. Between Sam and I, we tried just about everything possible. Finally, I hit upon the idea of using the GI Joe head as a dot on the "j" of the name. We put the head of a soldier on the packages relating to the Army series and a pilot's head on the Air Corps material and so on. They seemed to really like that idea in conjunction with the color-coding, so, other than condensing the gothic typeface a bit to get more display space out of the narrow area we had to use, that logo became the final.

The line was getting really large. Finally we had just too many things that they wanted done yesterday. I had gone to school with an artist named George Eisenberg and I got him interested in this project. We subcontracted him to help us get the illustrations done as production deadlines approached.

**The GI Joe logo as rendered for sample boxes at Toy Fair 1964.**

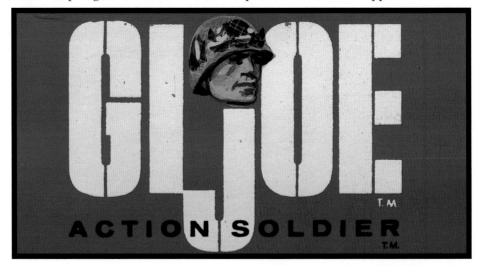

GEORGE EISENBERG: I served aboard a destroyer, the USS *La Vallette* DD 448, during World War II, and my vessel saw more than its share of action. We were almost sunk twice and I was wounded once.

After one particularly perilous battle off Guadalcanal, my captain recommended me for a line officer's commission and asked what I'd be interested in. I had been keeping a detailed sketch diary of my tour of duty, so I took a deep breath and asked for a specialist's rank as Combat Artist. To my astonishment, he said, "Why not?" Alas, that particular captain was transferred soon afterward and nothing came of it. Still, I maintained my sketch diary while off duty and tried to keep my pencil steady as the big guns fired.

My sketching during wartime gave me a good "shorthand" as far as creating the final pose for an action sequence. The gestures and sense of movement were things I'd seen in real life, and the war-learned memory of action and reaction under fire would one day serve me well.

During the sixties we had a local telephone operator who I knew very well, so I'd lift up the phone and say, "Hi, Dotty." I'd then ask her if she knew of any people who looked like Gregory Peck, around twenty-two years old, who would like to model for me. I got a lot of GI Joe models that way; she was very helpful. One of my most-used models, Pat Gorman, was likely found through Dotty.

Getting the necessary equipment and accessories was often part of the search. If a model had the costume I needed, so much the better.

DON LEVINE: As I left for my first of what would be many business trips to Hong Kong, the GI Joe name weighed heavily on my mind. It was very important that we secure the rights to this name in the toy world in order to avoid knock-offs from all directions—another hole in the market. We had determined that there was a GI Joe candy bar and comic book, and in the mid-forties there was a tin product, but, amazingly, no *toys* were using the name. We seemed to be clear as of 1963.

One of the points Hasbro's attorney, Elliot Salter, made to me was that in order to trademark the name you have to ship that name in the finished package interstate. That indicates that you're doing it; you're actually carrying on interstate commerce under a certain title.

"So ship some stuff," Salter said to me. What stuff? We weren't in production with GI Joe yet. "Put any doll in GI Joe packaging and ship it," he says. So, just before I went overseas, I started to put together little shipments and send them to my friend Mel Globus, who owned the Attleboro Tire and Appliance Company in Massachusetts—right across the state line. I would send the boxes and Mel would sign the receipt that I'd in turn give to Elliot for his trademark case. To this day Mel Globus laughs and says, "You couldn't have done it without me and my gas station."

I was also concerned about somebody copying our figure. One of the first things I did upon arriving in Hong Kong was visit a lawyer about protecting ourselves from duplication. In Hong Kong—in the early days—if you were knocked off on a toy or anything, you told the Chinese police about it and they went into the factory that was copying you and busted up all the tools and machinery and hit the people over the head. There was no crime in Hong Kong. The lawyer over there told me we could get the name protected without difficulty, but he warned that, as far as the GI Joe figure was concerned, we weren't merely trying to trademark a registered, patented toy; this was the human body. Who can claim they own rights to the human body? Within days of its production the Chinese would copy it.

There was one way to stop them, though. This lawyer suggested that we do something distinctive with the face and body so we—and the courts—could easily recognize a direct knock-off and stop it at customs. Right then and there I knew how to make Joe truly one of a kind.

From the shipboard
sketchbook of
George Eisenberg.

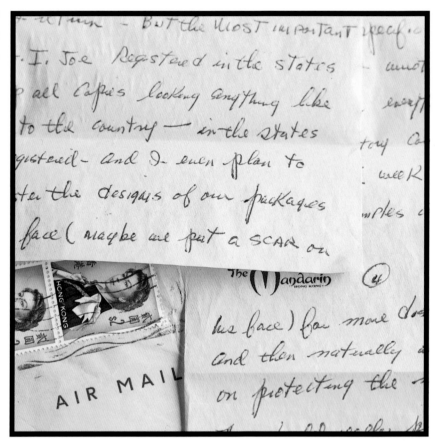

LETTER FROM DON LEVINE IN HONG KONG TO SAM SPEERS,
NOVEMBER 17, 1963:

*Just returned this weekend from Tokyo and Osaka, Japan, where we have been
for several days—met with lawyers there to try and protect Joe.*

*Call Elliot Salter and give him the attached pamphlet I got here—he and
I are going to have a long talk when I return. I've visited with the Hong Kong
lawyers and also in Osaka. Hong Kong seems very difficult to register our
name but in Japan we're maybe OK! He and I have to really talk when I
return—But the most important thing is to get GI Joe registered in the States
and then we can keep all copies looking anything like ours from coming into
the country—in the States we MUST get it registered. And I even plan to try
and register the designs and packages plus our man's face (maybe we put a scar
on his face) for more distinctness.*

SAM SPEERS: While Don geared up the overseas factories to produce sewn items, heads, and accessories, Walter Hansen and I continued to deal with the articulated body.

One of the things about Barbie and Ken was they were smooth. I wasn't too excited about making a doll for boys, so if I was going to do it I wanted it to be very masculine and robotlike. There was no harm in showing joints or articulation because once you cover them with a uniform it's all hidden. The changing and retaining of position was more important than anything else.

Don was very much a perfectionist, and he said he'd rather not see the connectors and joints. But, from an engineering standpoint, I had to get friction on all joints, and I had to do it quickly. Every joint had to contain resistance to motion of surfaces that touch.

We took apart the artist's mannequin that started it all, and boy did we examine it. Inside it had what were called expansion springs; you give that to a child and it's not going to last.

I'd wake up in the middle of the night and walk around the house wondering, "How am I going to get this thing done? How will I get him to stand up? How do I get his arms to stay in one spot when you have him hold a rifle or grasp a grenade?"

It came down to *slamming* those rivets, really pressing those plastic parts against each other. Then we had to find a way to hold it all together. Elastic bands were fine, but they just get old and break. For some reason I knew about elastic braid, and there was a company not one mile from our plant that was in the elastic braid business—Rhode Island Textile. The correct friction and that elastic braid made GI Joe work.

The ring-threaded adaptors used at the ankle, wrist, biceps, and knee turned out to be a wonderful innovation. They went into the holes made for them and were hard to pull out.

We had to make sure GI Joe could sit, and there was no question that a ball-hip would be involved. As a kid I'd taken apart golf balls, and I remembered that the little rubber sphere inside seemed perfect. David Molter, a guy down in our purchasing department, came from U.S. Rubber and I knew they made golf balls. He gave me a name there and I got myself about twenty of those little balls. They had great friction on them; they were just perfect. We put them on the drill press and got the braid through them. GI Joe could sit.

JANET DOWNING: Walter and Sam would make molded pieces of body as they went along to test how they worked together. They were learning to make polyvinyl flourochloride, whatever that is, to make the sample molds. It's very tricky, putting those chemicals together with the right timing, and sometimes the thing would explode. There was wretched awful acrid smoke

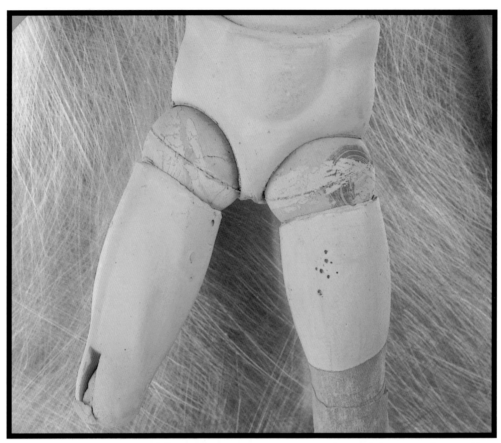

left in the air if the combination wasn't just right, and there's Walter, puffing on a cigarette the whole time!

DON LEVINE: We needed to make a presentation in Hong Kong to the big shipping magnates Wheelock-Marden, who were Hong Kong Industrial's partner. In order for Hong Kong Industrial to do our production, Wheelock-Marden had to invest some money—so naturally they needed to be convinced that we and our product were a good risk.

We went into a very stale-looking building and were shown to a giant conference room where tea was served at a huge teakwood table, biggest thing I'd ever seen. I got up and made my presentation to these very stiff-looking Brits, and the chairman said, "Thank you very much, gentlemen," and we walked out.

I said, "Well, we're going to have to find another group. Those guys were sucking lemons in there." But the next day Hong Kong Industrial called and announced that they had got all the money they needed. We were going forward.

There was always a lot of work to do while in Hong Kong and Japan, but it was quite an experience for a young man to travel in the Orient at that time. Hong Kong wasn't at all like it is today. In the early sixties there was still a "frontier" environment, with dirt roads and boards for sidewalks. The dredge for the harbor was so deep that aircraft carriers, destroyers, and battleships were right up against the dock; guys would step off right onto Main Street. We'd look out of our window in the Hong Kong Hilton and see the Communist guns on top of the hills facing down on us.

Since the American government wasn't allowed to deal with a Communist government, there were strict trade restrictions on goods made in Communist China. In Hong Kong, warehouses called "go downs" stored products imported from China for two or three weeks until they could stamp "Made in Hong Kong" on them. Nan loved the beautiful hand-rolled and fashioned handkerchiefs, so I'd pick up fifty or so that I'd get for a half-buck apiece.

Merrill came over in late November of 1963. I remember one Saturday morning getting up to go to the factory and seeing a newspaper slipped under our door: "Kennedy Assassinated." We woke up and looked out our window into the harbor and saw all of the flags at half mast on our U.S. ships.

Everyone remembers where they were when John Kennedy was killed. We were half a world away from home. Merrill tried to get through to his wife, Sylvia, on the phone, but lines were jammed all over the world.

We went down for breakfast on that terrible day, and our waiter asked us straight out, "Why do Americans have guns? No guns in Hong Kong; just the police and military." We couldn't answer him.

## Part 5

# Toy Fair 1964 and Beyond

**D**ON LEVINE: I came back to Pawtucket to finalize all of the artwork and accessories for my return to Japan and Hong Kong. Meanwhile, the factories were getting ready.

The clothing, hand-painted heads, and box-printing would be done overseas. The body and final assembly of packages would be done in our own plants. In order to have production going at a rate that would allow us to ship orders following Toy Fair in February of 1964, I'd have to return to the Orient with all the final artwork and samples we needed for seventy-five separate products. Furthermore, we had to mock up pre-production material to show at Toy Fair so the buyers had something to look at. They certainly weren't going to place orders based on the mere *idea* of a moveable fighting man with an array of accessories.

It was crunch time; an enormous amount of details to attend to and an enormous amount of pressure—while at the same time dealing with all of various other products in Hasbro's line for 1964. I was seeing endless amounts of GI Joe material that needed fine-tuning or approvals.

SAM SPEERS: Everyone in the department had the freedom to contribute to brainstorming accessories and combinations. There was no selfishness; it was cooperation. I'd been in the service for two years and I knew what the military was all about. Obviously, everyone had a different uniform, they all had different guns, they needed hammocks in the Navy and sleeping bags in the Army. We'd try to fill up each package so they all had equal perceived value.

JERRY EINHORN: We got our hands on a couple of actual military manuals. That manual would go into every package, and I wrote copy to tell kids what was included and how to use it.

DON LEVINE: Sam and his department had finished the figure, and I was a little concerned at first sight. Unclothed, he had a barrel chest, skinny legs and rivets all over the place. But when we got a uniform on him and put him through his paces, I began to see that we truly had a "fully poseable man of action." He could stand and sit, crouch and recline; there'd never been anything like it.

In looking over the small details, I caught a tiny error; the thumb on the right hand had an inverted thumbnail, placing the nail where the fingerprint should be. I pointed it out to Walter Hansen and he apologized, "Sorry, Don— I've been doing so many darn little details that I slipped up there. I'll fix it

*An early test head before hand-painting. GI Joe came with blonde, brunette, red, or brown hair and blue or brown eyes.*

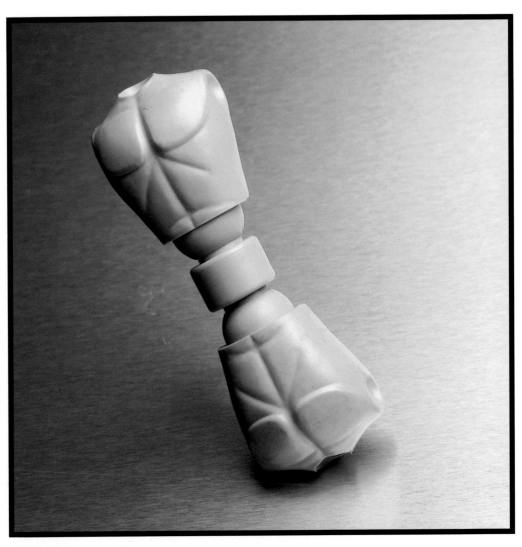

before tooling." I was reminded of my conversation with the lawyer in Hong Kong and said, "No problem, Walter. Let's leave it that way."

That thumbnail would act as our identifying mark. A mapmaker will sometimes add a nonexistent street with his name attached; if another map comes out with that same street on it, he knows he's been copied. Now we had a scar to protect the face and an error on the hand to individualize our body.

It wasn't much more than a year after we introduced GI Joe that this thumbnail helped us nab a knock-off. Jerry Einhorn always kept an eye out for toys that might be copies of ours. One day he called and said, "Don, that thumb of yours is on this 'Fighting Yank' toy." He brought it in, and he was right; Mego had evidently copied our figure and changed the face slightly. The thumbnail was right where we'd put it, though. There was no way they had created their figure without copying GI Joe; the District Court of New York found in our favor.

HUBERT P. O'CONNOR: Upon approval of the figure I bought sample molds from a local firm and immediately found that we'd face enormous difficulty in matching all the skin tones and textures. The chest was blow-molded and had to match the injection-molded limbs, and then everything had to match the head that was made overseas. It was up to quality control to get a fix on all the colors and ensure everything matched before we did a significant run.

**Early paint tests of the production GI Joe head.**

DON LEVINE: We confronted a lot of waste and a general lack of labor-saving thinking in the Hong Kong factories when production started up, contrary to the tight and efficient operations they soon became. My associate and I found ourselves having to constantly check and correct procedures and details that we considered obvious.

Since Merrill was very concerned about holding down our overseas costs, a "good cop, bad cop" routine was worked out for negotiating prices with vendors. On more than one occasion we'd be seated across the table from our factory representatives with price lists on our laps, and an item would come in at, say, $1.03, when we knew we had to get it at 97 cents. The Japanese had a phrase—"never happen"—that they'd start repeating when they didn't want to budge. The "bad cop" would jump up—"Did you hear what he just said? That's it!"—and storm out of the room, slamming the door. Meanwhile, the "good cop"—nearly always me—sat there innocent as can be, ready to pick up the pieces. We'd meet later at the hotel bar and critique each others performance. This arrangement didn't always work, but often enough we'd get our price.

It was a lot of tough, long hours, but we finally felt sure that we'd have product ready to ship soon after Toy Fair. That is, if the buyers bit. To hedge our bet, Merrill Hassenfeld had budgeted $25,000 for a sales film to be produced by the Bruns ad agency. We'd show it to our sales force at the pre-Toy Fair meeting so everyone would be clear on the concept.

## The GI Joe Sales Film

**Shown at the 1964 Toy Fair to the Hasbro sales force and potential buyers, this $25,000 presentation featured the following stirring narration over footage showing just how much fun a fully articulated soldier can be.**

GI Joe reporting for duty, sir!

Since the beginning of time children have always played soldier with wooden swords, broomstick rifles, with cast lead soldiers, with plastic miniatures. But none of these had the ring of authenticity. None of these gave a boy the feeling that he was playing real soldier. Give a boy an army field manual, and his fanciful imagination will carve reality out of thin air.

To make a boy's dream come true, Hasbro is proud to present GI Joe, America's moveable fighting man—the most realistic soldier anyone has ever seen. Imagine, GI Joe stands almost a foot tall. A soldier big enough to really play with.

But look—GI Joe doesn't just stand; he kneels, he lifts his arms to fire a rifle. He can charge or he can sit down and rest. He can throw a grenade or crouch in a foxhole. He can perform every action of a soldier because Hasbro's GI Joe has twenty-one moveable parts. His head turns. His arms move. He bends his elbow. His

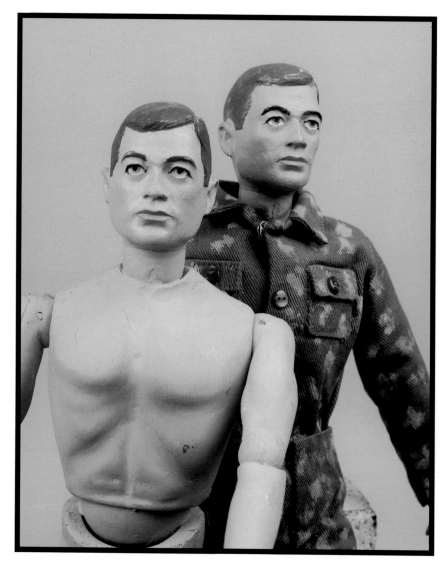

Two of the early hand samples used to "pre-sell" the GI Joe concept to buyers. At this point, the body sculpting and articulation were nearly finalized.

wrists move. He can turn from left to right. He can move his legs. He can bend his knees. He can even turn his feet. Twenty-one moveable parts. GI Joe brings a new kind of action realism to playing soldier. Look at his face. Not just an artist's fancy, this is the face of GI Joe. Carefully designed from composite photographs of twenty medal of honor winners.

What about his uniforms? They're just uniforms—just the *regulation* uniforms. Just the *authentic* uniforms of the quartermaster corps designed for the real life GI Joe. Fatigue uniforms, battle dress, MP uniforms. Whatever the action, the real uniform.

But wait. We're getting ahead of our story. Take a look at GI Joe's battle gear. A new kind of action realism in playing soldier. All of his gear—from canteen and mess kit to .30-caliber machine gun, from entrenching tools and field pack to communication equipment—is all regulation gear designed from official army and navy blueprints; and each piece of gear is scaled to size so that it fits. The canteen cover fits over the canteen.

→

UNDERWATER
DEMOLITION

COMMUNICATIONS

PARA MARINE
JUMPER

GI JOE
ACTION SAILOR

GI JOE

GI JOE

GI JOE
ACTION MARINE

ATTACK SERIES

MILITARY POLICE

DRESS PARADE

**Hasbro archive photo of painted package mock-ups used for the 1964 sales film.**

SAM PETRUCCI: In those days there was no way to reproduce art like we can today; silk-screening was the only way to get everything looking like production. I had a friend in the business who had shown me how to do it, so I was able to prepare packages for showing at Toy Fair and for the film they were doing. The Hasbro art department gave us blank, flat boxes, and I dupli-

The canteen clips on to the cartridge belt, and the cartridge belt fits over the uniform. This is GI Joe Action Soldier.

Here is the basic package; and an exciting package it is, with beautiful four-color action illustrations. But Hasbro gives to the boys of America more than just a sensational new kind of soldier. Hasbro introduces a whole new concept in playing soldier. To go with GI Joe Action Soldier there is box after box of regulation military gear, different kinds of uniforms, all sorts of battle equipment. Authentic GI Joe material with everything from combat to bivouac. From MP to command post. Helmets, rifles, tents, flags, sandbags, machine guns. Everything carefully reproduced down to the last detail.

But this is just the beginning. In this giant new concept Hasbro brings to the youth of America not only GI Joe Action Soldier but also GI Joe Action Marine, GI Joe Action Sailor and GI Joe Action Pilot. Four GI Joes, four different services.

cated all of our type designs, illustrations, and other details onto them.

JERRY EINHORN: Thresher and Petrucci were finalizing the artwork and we had to get the labels printed and the boxes made; we were rushing. Don and I had to go up to Harold Thresher's studio, and we went in Don's station wagon. Don never told me—this was in January, with the coldest day of the year—that the heater didn't work in his car. And let me tell you, it was cold when I was in Korea, but this was colder. We froze. Coming back it was late at night—we were with them until seven, eight at night—and we were driving back down Route 1 and we were so cold we had to stop off two or three times just to get a cup of coffee to warm up before we got into the car again and drove home. I never let Don forget about that one.

DON LEVINE: Toy Fair was held yearly in New York City. It's the event in the toy industry where all the major companies unveil their new products for the jobbers and buyers who decide what goes on the shelves at stores all over the country. These buyers consult with our sales representatives and place orders for what they think will be in demand for the coming year. In other words, if you want kids to be impressed by a new toy, these are the people you have to inspire first.

I wanted to present GI Joe in a magnificent way to the two thousand or so industry people who would come through the Hasbro showroom. I wanted to start a buzz: "Hey, you should get over to see what Hasbro has."

SAM SPEERS: I always enjoyed playing with soldiers outside as a kid. It was most fun when you could put them in realistic settings. One day Don came up to me and said, "We've got to have a display for New York—a diorama." "One for each service?" I asked, and he agreed. I told him we'd need some money, and he took care of it.

The time immediately preceding Toy Fair is very stressful; you're always setting up the night before the buyers come in. I went to downtown Providence

This is GI Joe Action Marine. Uniformed in camouflage fatigues with all sorts of exciting marine equipment. Here is everything from paratrooper to communications. From dress parade to beachhead assault. Parachute packs, carbines, flame throwers, camouflage communication gear, helmets and flags. GI Joe Action Marine brings a new kind of action realism to playing soldier.

To go with GI Joe Action Sailor there are these exciting Navy packages. Equipment for sea rescue, for frogman, for navy attack, and US Navy shore patrol. Children will be fascinated by the detail and the regulation equipment. Life preservers, scuba suits, scuba tanks, swim fins, complete shore-patrol gear. GI Joe Action Sailor brings a new kind of action realism to playing soldier.

To go with GI Joe Action Pilot there are thrilling sets of Air Force equipment. Everything from scramble to survival and, of course, dress uniforms. High altitude helmets, flight suits, pad and clipboard, air vests, flare guns, all the gear necessary so that GI Joe Action Pilot can bring a new kind of action realism to playing soldier.

→

and had a plastics firm put together large Plexiglas square boxes. When those were completed and shipped to New York, we filled them with rocks, sand, and broken trees. I remember I took some stones from my wall at home to New York for the display. They ended up looking sensational.

HUBERT P. O'CONNOR: We took test samples from the GI Joe body molds at 11:00 P.M. on the night of the Liston-Patterson fight. We had gofers with ranch wagons parked outside the door, and all night long they made runs to New York. We didn't even have time to assemble anything—Sam and his crew were at the Toy Fair exhibit putting everything together.

DON LEVINE: These dioramas were monsters. For the Army scene, we had twenty or thirty Joes in a battle; for the Navy scene, a squadron of Joes were on the deck of a ship. We spent thousands and thousands on these things, and I made sure that when the designers set them up they featured the figures in all kinds of crazy poses, because that's what I wanted to sell—you could never before do things like that.

For Toy Fair, Hasbro used to rent the Barbizon Plaza Hotel theater to make presentations to the sales force, ad agency, marketing; everyone involved with selling and promoting the products for that particular year. In 1964, we used that opportunity to show the GI Joe sales film to everyone. Many of the sales reps hadn't even seen a GI Joe figure yet, and they really

**Ready for the wild blue yonder in the Scramble ensemble and Scramble Crash Helmet.**

**GI Joe Action Marine**

GI Joe. A concept so big it requires dozens of different packages ranging in retail price from $1 to $5. Fascinating sets of equipment so the boys of America will be able to play with GI Joe. And each package has an authentic field manual that shows all the equipment a boy can get. And each GI Joe has his own GI dog tag. Thousands of boys will start with one service, but other thousands will start with two GI Joes and even all four. Market research tests show that boys who have played with GI Joe want all four; and, with a full range of authentic equipment, the four-way GI Joe line builds into the greatest open-end merchandising program the boys market has had since the introduction of the electric train. GI Joe cannot live his service life and fight his playroom battles without the full range of equipment, which is built into all four categories and sold in beautiful and dramatic packages.

And to promote this revolutionary concept Hasbro will use the most strategic advertising campaign ever put behind a toy—a campaign planned not only to reach every boy in America but every adult. Plans call for

→

needed to watch this new kind of toy in action in order to get a sense of the huge scope of the line.

Merrill went around to all the sales people and personally repeated our mandate: "Don't you dare sell this as a doll. If I overhear you talking to a client about a doll, we're not shipping any GI Joe product to you! It's a soldier; an articulated, moving soldier!"

We had a private showing of the line at the Regency Hotel on Park Avenue for the same "buying fraternity" that we'd consulted so many months earlier when the project was in its infancy. Now the chips were down and the money

giant advertising and mammoth publicity. Advertising strategy that will use television as though this were truly a battle for the consumer's dollar. On the right flank, GI Joe on network television. On the left flank, GI Joe on spot television in your market. And right up the center, a GI Joe print campaign in comics, in newspapers, in magazines. Total advertising strategy. Exciting television commercials. Startling and dramatic print ads. A publicity campaign with stories already projected and in the works for America's leading magazines. An advertising strategy conceived and dedicated to but one purpose—to make every boy and every parent a part of the big parade to toy stores everywhere. To see and to buy . . .

GI Joe, America's moveable fighting man.

Hut two three four, hut two three four.

On the land, on the sea, and in the air. He's here in the wonderful world of toys, and Hasbro's got him.

GI JOE!

was spent. We got the same mixed-bag reaction, but it was clear as the week went on that they would at least buy the quantities necessary to test GI Joe in their stores.

JERRY EINHORN: Merrill had a suite in the Regency Hotel, and we would bring the whole GI Joe display in, all seventy-five packages, and set them up on racks to show the really big buyers. Not only to show it to them, but to pick their brains and get their input because these were the stores who had success with Barbie, and these are the guys who knew what they were looking for.

The big dean of the buyers, the buyer from Woolworth's, looked at it and said, "Do you have the patterns for this stuff so that you can get into it right away? Because you've got something great here." That was the clincher; we knew we had it.

DON LEVINE: We got through Toy Fair in good shape. Orders were placed in enough quantity that we knew GI Joe would be out there on the shelves for the public to decide for themselves—and they wouldn't begin to see product until July. We then had to wait for the response from larger retail chains that generally didn't take substantive orders until closer to their big selling season, which was—as it is now—the months preceding Christmas.

Silk-screened GI Joe Action Marine box as produced for the 1964 sales film. The red box at lower right was changed for actual production to contain figure illustrations in addition to the slogan "America's Moveable Fighting Man."

The problem we all lived with in the toy industry is that a company could not simply present an inexpensively raw idea for a new product at Toy Fair, sit back and count the orders they got for that particular item, then decide to manufacture the goods based on the feedback received from buyers. To be in a position to get a complex item like GI Joe to our customers on a timely basis, a substantial investment had to be made in advance. Merrill Hassenfeld used to warn me about the fact that you have to spend a lot of money before you realize you have a flop in the business, and that was never more true than in the case of GI Joe; Hasbro was on the line for $2 million in development and manufacturing costs by the time the first shipments of uniforms and accessories were in the final stages of preparation in the Orient. As was standard practice in the toy industry, we wouldn't see payment for any product we provided to our customers until the last few months of the year.

**The soldier's best friend, his general-purpose motor vehicle, 1965.**

As we got closer to our shipping date, the task of making sure every single piece of the GI Joe line was manufactured correctly lay before me. This meant attending to countless details as production samples began to come in over the spring and summer of 1964. Seams, buttons, colors; even the placement of individual items in the package had to be checked and re-checked.

MARGE McCRAE (Secretary to Don Levine): Don would dictate reams of information and corrections after they'd send us samples from the overseas factories. He would give them instructions on what we wanted, or we'd make up prototypes in Rhode Island which he would take to Hong Kong. Then the factory over there was supposed to duplicate them for us and then they'd send back samples to us of what they'd done. Don was so fussy about everything that it took a long time to get things exactly the way that would suit him before they went into production.

**The Soldiers of the World series featured accurate reproductions of the uniforms and accessories of Russian, Australian, British, French, German, and in this case, Japanese fighting men.**

I had to take hundreds and thousands of words, and we used Dictaphones in those days so I was a busy lady. We had problems every day in the week. We were always having problems. But I got a big thrill out of contacting Hong Kong and even talking to them on the telephone because I couldn't understand some of these Chinese people. Their accents were so strange. I can't even remember the names of

people we spoke to now, but I met
them because they came to Pawtucket
to visit the factory and everything.

Using the Telex we sent them
all this information, and they in turn
sent it back to us. There was a
twelve-hour delay in the time so
when we were working during the
day here in Rhode Island, that was
their night. Before I could go home
from work—we were supposed to
get out of work at five—I had to
make sure that all the dictation that
Don had given to me during the day
got transmitted to Hong Kong.
When they came to work in the
morning, all this information would
be waiting for them on their Telex
machine, and vice versa. They would
send a reply to us during their working day, and when we came into
work in the morning one of the first
things we had to do was go into the
room where the Telex machine was
and rip off the long yellow sheets

A hand-painted
Black soldier.

from the machine with the messages that they had sent to us so that we could
work on it. That was one of the most important parts of the job, I think.

DON LEVINE: By introducing seventy-five packages at Toy Fair, we were
successful in preventing other toy manufacturers from jumping on our
product by creating extra accessories we didn't have available; quite simply,
we'd made just about everything a soldier of any branch of the military could
possibly want.

By the same token, it would take some real imagination and ambition to
expand the GI Joe line in 1965. Even as I took off for the Orient to oversee
ongoing production of the 1964 line, I gave marching orders to my staff to
begin creating ideas for 1965.

In order to truly portray the full range of American GIs, we immediately
added a Black soldier. There was never any question; our Black soldier would
not be "GI Joe's friend" or some sort of sidekick. While the issue of civil rights
was emerging as a national hot point—Martin Luther King, Jr., had just won
the 1964 Nobel Peace Prize, and the country had been transfixed by his march

on Washington in 1963—we at Hasbro knew first and foremost that bravery and heroism were not limited to persons of any particular color or creed. It would simply have been illogical to create an Everyman who did not truly represent every man.

It was equally easy to decide that GI Joe needed a vehicle—of course, that meant reproducing the classic g. p.

**SAM SPEERS:** We had a library book—which I *still* have—called *Hail to the Jeep* by A. Wade Wells, and that book whet our appetite to do the vehicle. We got one from General Holland so Walter and Norman could measure the real thing.

I had always been fascinated with deep-sea divers. My first inspiration was the big helmet with the knobs and doors on it—it certainly

**With Barbie doing enormous business among America's little girls, Hasbro aimed squarely and exclusively at the male market.**

seemed like something we should add to the line. I told Don we could get GI Joe to submerge and then come to the surface by blowing air down a tube to his helmet for some play action. It ended up being a beautiful item and package with artwork by Harold Thresher.

**JERRY EINHORN:** We decided we were going to do an astronaut, but not just an astronaut uniform to put on a GI Joe—we were going to do the whole thing. The Mercury, which was our first space capsule, was the big deal at the time. John Glenn had recently done his first three orbits of the earth, our first man actually to go around the world in space. I contacted General Holland again and he put me on to Senator John O. Pastore, one of the senators from Rhode Island. I called his office and went to Washington, to the Pentagon—getting lost in the Pentagon is a story in itself; I'm lucky I'm here because I could still be walking those corridors—and I got to the NASA office where they were expecting me. To my relief, I could tell them what we were doing because GI Joe was no longer a secret.

"We want to do an astronaut, but not just a uniform for NASA—we want to actually injection mold a miniature spaceship of the sort John Glenn orbited in. And we're going to make it so that GI Joe can fit in it in a space

In crafting the Astronaut uniform for release in 1967, the Hasbro team created a snug, "space-worthy" seal between the collar and helmet at Levine's insistence.

A bicycle inner tube provided the ideal material for this preliminary mock-up of a wet suit.

Hands created for maximum utility, yet compact enough to fit through scale clothing.

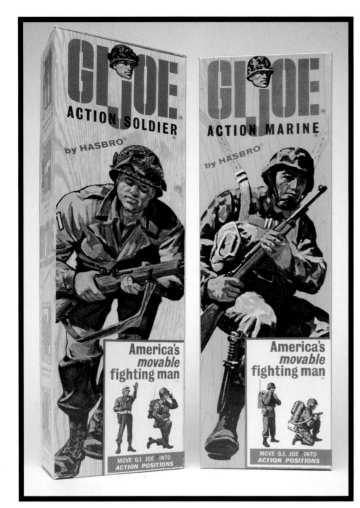

uniform. We'd like to put a 45-rpm record in there telling kids about space travel as well."

They thought that was a great idea. It just so happened that they had tapes of John Glenn that were recorded in the capsule during his three-hour flight. They said I could borrow the entire tape! My eyes lit up because I could take those three hours of tapes and edit them down to three minutes of John Glenn's voice during the lift-off, orbit, re-entry, and whatnot.

But we still needed the uniform. They took me into a part of their offices and there, standing up, was a six-foot mannequin dressed in a space uniform exactly like John Glenn's, with the bubble over the head and everything. I said, "Boy, if we could borrow that, that would be fantastic. We could actually make the uniform look exactly like that."

Well, they conferred; "Yeah, we'll let you borrow it."

I said, "I can't take it with me now, could you forward it to me?"

"Sure."

I left the Pentagon and flew back to Rhode Island. Everybody was happy with what I got; the tapes were fantastic. Two weeks later a truck pulls up and they had put this six-foot astronaut, dressed in the uniform with the bubble over his head, in a plain pine box. Looked like a coffin. This was brought up into Sam Speers's area, where Sam unhinges it and opens it up and there's this mannequin looking up at him with the uniform on! Well, that was great.

Sam put the cover back on. About a day later Merrill Hassenfeld wanders into Sam's area looking around—"How you doing, boys?"—and he sees this coffinlike box on the floor. He goes over and just lifts the cover, and then he drops it, because there's this body staring back at him in a space uniform! We thought the man was going faint. He started to laugh—he kept bringing everybody in to look at it.

DON LEVINE: Even as I coordinated the exciting new GI Joe material we were planning for 1965, our initial material hadn't yet been put before the real judge

One of the most
aesthetically pleasing and
startlingly functional of
the GI Joe accessory sets,
the 1965 Deep Sea Diver
featured a rubberized suit,
air hoses, and everything
from a turnable red valve
handle on its helmet . . .

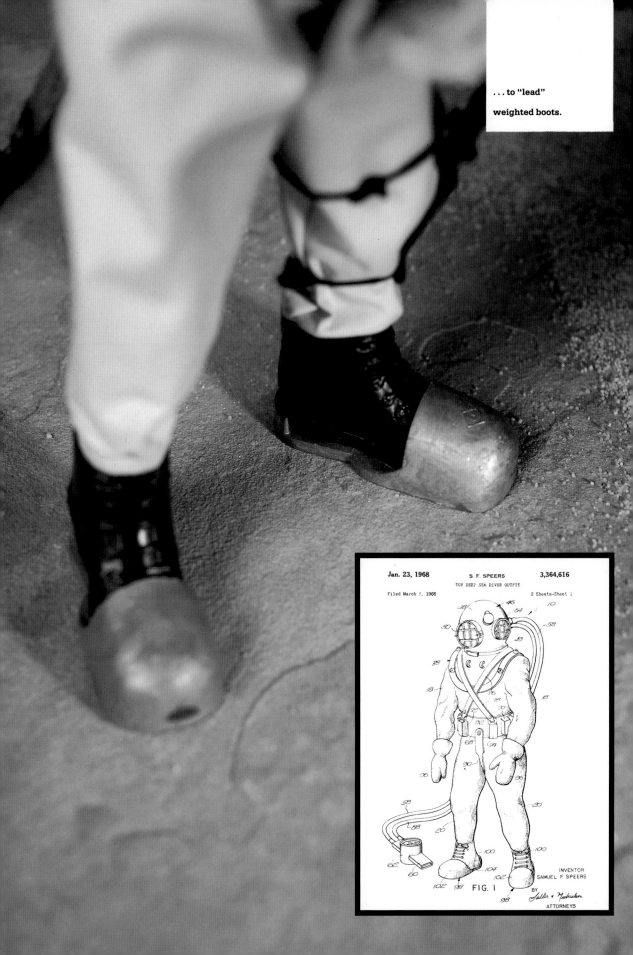

. . . to "lead"

weighted boots.

Jan. 23, 1968        S. F. SPEERS        3,364,616

TOY DEEP SEA DIVER OUTFIT

Filed March 7, 1966                    2 Sheets-Sheet 1

FIG. I

INVENTOR
SAMUEL F. SPEERS

BY

ATTORNEYS

An array of small illustrations created to adorn the side panels of prototype GI Joe figure packages.

## THEN...MARCH 1945

G. I. Joe broke the war wide open in March twenty-one years ago. After smashing through the Siegfried Line, G. I. Joe drove his armor to the Rhine. The Ninth Armored Division speeding to the town of Remagen found a bridge intact and made a surprise crossing. Further south General Patton with slashing speed and audacity slipped quietly across the Rhine on pontoons under cover of darkness and sent his spearhead division, the Fourth Armored, in a bold and flashing attack toward Frankfurt and the Main River. G. I. Joe's spring offensive was rolling!

# G.I.JOE®*
# IS ALWAYS
# UP
# FRONT

As this trade ad illustrates, Hasbro aligned GI Joe with America's collective memory of the last "good" war, World War II.

# NOW...MARCH 1966

In March 1966, Hasbro's G. I. Joe* opened his own spring offensive at the Toy Fair in New York with an amazing new expanded concept—the greatest development ever known in the field of playing soldier.

G. I. Joe, Action Soldier*, Action Marine*, Action Sailor* and Action Pilot*—introduced magnificent new uniforms and equipment—new ways to build battlegrounds—with new troops, new allies and new enemies!

Massive television fire-power on Network and Spot, day after day and week after week, will bring you business that will help you build the most profitable spring you ever had.

Get your share of Hasbro action!

**HASBRO**

**G. I. JOE* DIVISION, HASSENFELD BROS., INC., PAWTUCKET, RHODE ISLAND**
*Trademark of Hassenfeld Bros., Inc. Reg. U.S. Patent Office

# G.I. JOE ™

## ACTION SOLDIER ™

# PUNCH OUT

### AUTHORIZED EDITION

### ACTION SAILOR ™

### ACTION MARINE ™

### ACTION PILOT ™

WHITMAN PUBLISHING COMPANY
RACINE, WISCONSIN

and jury—the buying public. Heartening as Toy Fair was, we wouldn't really know what we'd gotten ourselves into until actual sales figures could be examined.

By summer our initial GI Joe product was finally getting on store shelves across the country. In August, Larry O'Daly, head of advertising and promotion, began running a commercial on New York's WPIX-TV once a day.

This was it; our labor of the past year was now on the line. My staff and I were secure in the knowledge that we'd done our absolute best work possible. Everyone had extended themselves to their limits in order to create the finest toy we had ever seen.

But—would the kids want our soldier?

The answer came quickly; in one week, GI Joe was sold out all over the New York area! Between August and September, selected stores across the country began stocking Joe and his accessories supported by TV ads on NBC—just one spot a week—and found themselves sold out nearly immediately. "Jobbers," the wholesale buyers who supplied product to stores all over America, began contacting our sales representatives for re-orders to keep up with consumer demand. GI Joe was an unqualified hit. Forget about worrying whether people will buy it; our new problem was getting the product made fast enough! Eventually a separate division for GI Joe had to be formed in order to handle the volume of orders coming in.

Now we needed to communicate our urgency in Hong Kong—it would be devastating to end up under-supplied as demand heated up. I took another trip to the Orient in order to light a fire under our representative at Hong Kong Industrial, T.S. Lowe. Hong Kong Industrial was owned by Wheelock-Marden, so we took an entire presentation to their offices, showed the whole GI Joe line and television commercial, and hoped that this gigantic company would recognize the need to push Hong Kong Industrial towards double and

More than $2.5 million was budgeted to promote the launch of Hasbro's fighting man. Full page ads in comic books were especially effective.

One of the many licensed products to emerge during GI Joe's first year, a punch-out book published by Whitman.

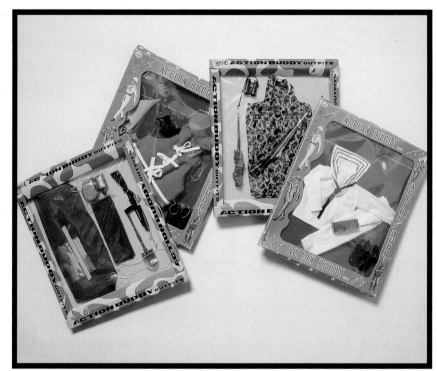

As predicted by Don Levine, the competition rushed in with inferior copies and "knock-offs" of GI Joe within months of his appearance in stores. In this case, "Jose" was created from a copy of GI Joe's body and even featured Hasbro's artwork and packaging concept.

triple production rates. As it turns out, John Marden himself walked into the meeting and was fascinated by what he saw; he was, in fact, unaware that one of his factories was making GI Joe and his accessories!

Needless to say, Wheelock-Marden quickly recognized that they had a potential goldmine and gave GI Joe high priority status. At the same time, several additional factories were located to handle overflow so Hasbro could keep orders filled and store shelves stocked.

Perhaps the most significant signal convincing us that we'd created something special occurred on a December day in 1964 when the Pawtucket Post Office notified Hasbro that they would no longer deliver mail to our offices. That same month we'd started the Official GI Joe Fan Club; for fifty cents each new member received an equipment catalog, an ID card, a membership certificate, a letter from "Col. Pat Lawrence," an iron-on transfer, and an official GI Joe dog tag. It seems the weight of thousands of quarters was just too much for the local mail truck.

Every genuine GI Joe product bore a seal of authenticity.

INSIST ON
AUTHENTIC
GI JOE
EQUIPMENT

Photograph used as box art for 1969 Danger of the Depths set.

# Epilogue

—

**DON LEVINE:** I've often described the early days of developing GI Joe as a lonely road. We were, after all, a very small group of people sweating out the details of a toy that common sense said wouldn't be accepted in the marketplace. We had no template to follow, no precedent to look to as a reference, certainly no guarantee of success, and no one to blame but ourselves if the product bombed. Maybe, above all, we simply had no "common sense."

What we did have, however, was a shared passion for the creation of a product we believed in. We proceeded from the notion that nothing was out of the question for GI Joe. "What the mind can conceive, the hand can create," is what I used to say; and I was surrounded by craftspeople with the pride and extraordinary ability necessary to carry out that philosophy. I couldn't wait to get to work every morning.

We also had a remarkable boss in the person of Merrill Hassenfeld, without whom there would be no GI Joe. To say that Merrill was highly regarded as a corporate and community leader is a gross understatement. While a shrewd and no-nonsense businessman, Merrill knew his employees and could enjoy a conversation with anyone, from the front office to the loading dock. He would take time to call Nan regularly during my many long trips overseas to make sure everything was okay while she was alone with our small children. Hasbro felt like an extended family under his leadership. He engendered trust and loyalty in everyone who knew him. In turn, he trusted us.

I'm proud to say that Merrill's trust has been amply rewarded. We were ambitious, but we couldn't have predicted the astounding success we had with GI Joe. As a product, it met and exceeded our wildest expectations and helped set Hasbro on a course toward the international stature it now enjoys. As a cultural phenomena, it took on a life of its own.

Nobody thought for a moment that our action soldier would become a fixture in the childhoods of so many people. I've been a guest at a couple of GI Joe collector's conventions, and it's enormously gratifying—and a bit humbling—to meet and talk to so many people for whom GI Joe was an integral part of their lives. I see fathers explaining to their children how they used to create action-filled worlds in their basements, rec rooms, and backyards. And since GI Joe has always been a man of his times adapting to a changing world, it's especially wonderful to see parents and children sharing enthusiasm for "their" GI Joe—whether a sixties military man, seventies bearded Adventure Team leader, a late-seventies Super Joe, or a smaller "Real American Hero" of the eighties and nineties—across the generation gap.

What started as a lonely road has become a wonderful community experience. The story of GI Joe has come full circle, and it's anything but over.

Ready for action in an ensemble created by combining the Combat Field Jacket and Combat Rifle Sets. A boy could begin his collection—in this case, a GI Joe Action Soldier figure and two carded accessory packages—for just over $10.

# Acknowledgments

—

**Photographs**

Pgs. 34, 35, 42, 72, 75, 76, 81, 82, 92 by Chris Becker;

Pgs. 10, 16, 26, 31, 40, 62, 69, 77, 80, back cover/upper right by Jim Egan;

Front cover photography by John William Lund;

Pgs. 20, 32, 33, 44, 45, 47, 49, 50, 51, 60, 65, 66, 67, 86–87, back cover/lower left by Brian Malloy;

Photos on pages 34–35, 42, and 75 are used here courtesy of Kalmbach Publishing.

—

The authors wish to offer special thanks to Hasbro employees past and present for their help and cooperation. Many of the people who shared their stories herein also contributed one of a kind archival material from their own collections for our usage.

Also, we owe a debt of gratitude to GI Joe collectors and enthusiasts all over the country who offered valuable input and the loan of many GI Joe figures and accessories for use in this book. Jeff Kilian located many of the original GI Joe package artists while researching articles of his own for numerous collector magazines and allowed us to photograph pieces from his collection. Other contributors of figures, accessories, and archival material were Joe Desris, Cotswold Collectibles, Dale Womer of the Hobby Lobby, Harold Fowler, Brian Savage, Kirk Bozigian, Vinnie D'Alleva, Paul Ivy, the Toy Wizard, and Jim Bzdawka.

Also, thanks to Jerilyn Miller Lowe for her promotional energy; Dionne Blaha, Bo Kanarek, and Julie LaFountain for transcribing above and beyond the call of duty; and Matt Lizak for his great package design.

Lastly, we're grateful to our editor, Jeffrey Schulte, and everyone at Chronicle Books for weathering the twists and turns that popped up with regularity throughout production of this Masterpiece Edition book and figure. We were able to realize our vision because Chronicle agrees that "what the mind can conceive, the hand can create."

—

**Bibliography**

GI Joe comic books:

© Ziff-Davis Publishing Company, New York, New York

© DC Comics, New York, New York

Fowler, Harold. *Field Manual for Collecting GI Joe 1963–1969*. Los Alamitos, CA: Pen and Quill Publishers, 1992.

Kilian, Jeff, and Charles Griffith. *Tomart's Price Guide to GI Joe Collectibles*. Dayton, Ohio: Tomart Publications, 1993.

"The Story of GI Joe: Old Taboo, New Market," *Sales Management*, October 15, 1965, pg. 74.